OSPREY COMBAT AIRCRAFT •90

AV-8B HARRIER II UNITS OF OPERATIONS *DESERT SHIELD* AND *DESERT STORM*

SERIES EDITOR: TONY HOLMES

OSPREY COMBAT AIRCRAFT • 90

AV-8B HARRIER II UNITS OF OPERATIONS *DESERT SHIELD* AND *DESERT STORM*

LON NORDEEN

OSPREY
PUBLISHING

Front Cover
On the morning of 17 January 1991, Maj Gen Royal Moore, Commanding General, 3rd Marine Aircraft Wing, called Col John Bioty Jr, CO of Marine Air Group (MAG) 13 (Forward) at King Abdul Aziz Naval Base, Saudi Arabia, and asked 'What is your status?' He added, 'We have an OV-10 reporting Iraqi shelling in the Khafji area'. Moore then said, 'Launch the ready Harriers'. Maj Richard C Branch, XO of VMA-311 (the first AV-8B squadron to arrive in theatre for Operation *Desert Shield*), was the alert duty officer. He, along with Capts Nelson Alberts, Frank Smith and Dino Peros, took off at 0740 hrs, flew northeast over the water and rendezvoused with the Forward Air Controller (Airborne) (FAC(A)) in an OV-10 Bronco surveillance aircraft that was monitoring the Iraqi shelling.

The weather over the target area was mixed, with an 8000-ft cloud deck. The OV-10 crew marked the entrenched 122 mm artillery battery with a white phosphorous rocket and Maj Branch, flying AV-8B BuNo 163664 'Tomcat 06', swept in from the water in a twenty-degree dive attack and dropped two Mk 83 1000-lb bombs on the first pass. His wingman and the other section, led by Capt Dino Peros, also bombed the artillery positions. Since there was no AAA or missile fire, Maj Branch and his pilots made additional bombing passes and several strafing runs, using up their full load of bombs and 25 mm cannon shells as they neutralised the artillery position and stopped the bombardment.

This was the first strike flown by the AV-8B Harrier II in *Desert Storm* and, after 20 years of service, signalled the combat debut for US Marine Corps Harriers (*Cover artwork by Gareth Hector using a model supplied by Milviz*)

First published in Great Britain in 2011 by Osprey Publishing
Midland House, West Way, Botley, Oxford, OX2 0PH
44-02 23rd Street, Suite 219, Long Island City, NY, 11101, USA

E-mail; info@ospreypublishing.com

Osprey Publishing is part of the Osprey Group

A CIP catalogue record for this book is available from the British Library

ISBN: 978 1 84908 444 4
e-book ISBN: 978 1 84908 445 1

Edited by Tony Holmes
Page design by Tony Truscott
Cover Artwork by Gareth Hector
Aircraft Profiles by Jim Laurier
Index by Alan Thatcher
Originated by United Graphic Pte Ltd
Printed in China through Bookbuilders

11 12 13 14 15   10 9 8 7 6 5 4 3 2 1

Osprey Publishing is supporting the Woodland Trust, the UK's leading woodland conservation charity by funding the dedication of trees.

www.ospreypublishing.com

CONTENTS

INTRODUCTION

US Marine Corps units always deploy as a combined arms force with a mix of ground, command and control, combat support and aviation assets united within a Marine Air-Ground Task Force (MAGTF). Units differ in size and composition depending upon the task and forces available. The smallest MAGTF generally deployed is a Marine Expeditionary Unit (MEU), which includes a battalion landing team, supporting units, a composite helicopter squadron and often after 1986 a detachment of six AV-8B Harrier IIs. These forces are embarked in three or more US Navy amphibious ships, plus supporting naval escorts, and deployed around the world to react to a mix of missions from peacekeeping to major warfare.

The largest Marine Corps fighting force prepared to deal with a serious situation such as the Iraqi invasion of Kuwait in 1990 is a Marine Expeditionary Force (MEF). A MEF includes one or more Marine divisions, an aircraft wing and an associated force service support group, which can operate from amphibious ships and/or land sites. The 3rd Marine Aircraft Wing (MAW) deployment to support 1st Marine Expeditionary Force's efforts to liberate Kuwait included three squadrons of AV-8B Harrier IIs operating from King Abdul Aziz Naval Base in Saudi Arabia. At sea, one and one-third squadrons of AV-8Bs supported the 4th and 5th Marine Expeditionary Brigades from USS *Nassau* (LHA-4) and USS *Tarawa* (LHA-1).

Acknowledgements
Many individuals supported the development of this volume, including Dr Fred Allison, Hank Cole, David Isby, Dr Jim Ginther, Mary Joscelyn, Ben Kristy, Cdr Peter Mersky, Pat Mitts, Dr Charles Neimeyer and Vlado Zavich.

I would also like to thank the Marine Corps aviators from the following units;

MAG-13 (Forward) – Col John Bioty Jr (CO)
VMA-231 – Cols W R Jones (CO), Anton Nerad and Russell Sanborn, Lt Cols Donald E Fleming (XO) and Andrew Hall and Maj David Vosteen
VMA-311 – Lt Cols Dick White (CO), Cary Branch and Mike Hile
VMA-331 – Lt Col J W Fitzgerald (CO) and Cols Ben Hancock and Charles Hobaugh
VMA-513 – Lt Cols Thomas Carnesi and Georges LeBlanc
VMA-542 – Lt Col Theodore Herman (CO) and Col Art Tomassetti

AV-8B AND THE MAGTF

US Marine Corps aviation is different. All Marine aircrew are trained as infantry before they become aviators, and they are encouraged to fill the role of forward air controllers (FACs) at some stage in their career. The Marine Corps tactical aviation element has four major missions – air superiority, reconnaissance, interdiction and close air support. However, the focus has nearly always been on tactical support for ground operations and the Marine rifleman. By 1990 the Marine air-ground team had more than 70 years' experience ranging from the Dominican Republic and Haiti to Nicaragua, the Pacific in World War 2, Korea and Vietnam.

The US Department of Defense (DoD) identifies close air support (CAS) as 'air action against hostile forces which are in close proximity to friendly forces and which require detailed integration of each mission with fire and movement of these forces'. Practically speaking, that means understanding how ground forces operate, and significantly enhancing their effectiveness with air-delivered weapons.

During the World War 2 island-hopping campaign across the Pacific, Marine Corps aviation refined CAS tactics and techniques through the use of radio-equipped FACs deployed with infantry battalions, the employment of smoke and marker panels to indicate targets and the location of friendly troops and the delivery of munitions such as napalm.

In the post-World War 2 downsizing the Marine Corps faced a challenge to its existence, but the 1947 National Security Act defined the structure, size and focus of the post-war Marine Corps as follows;

'Not less than three combat divisions and three air wings, and provide fleet Marine forces of combined arms, together with supporting air components, for service with the fleet in the seizure and defence of advanced naval bases for the conduct of such land operations as may be essential to the prosecution of a naval campaign. In addition, the Marine Corps shall perform such other duties as the President may direct.'

Less than three years later the Marine Corps was deeply involved in the unexpected war in Korea, where CAS provided much needed

Representative examples from the Marine Corps light attack tactical aviation inventory from the early 1970s through to the 1990s fly together over Arizona's Western Desert. Maj Gen H S Hill, USMC explained to the US Congress the decision to buy the V/STOL Harrier as opposed to other systems like the A-4. 'In the Marine Corps air-ground team, we have struck a careful balance in the number and types of supporting arms to enable the Marine ground commander to effectively carry out his mission. Marines have pioneered close air support and devoted primary attention to improvements in development of close air support systems to include the V/STOL Harrier aircraft.' In the foreground is the TAV-8A from VMAT-203, next is an OA-4M two-seat forward observation aircraft, while the jet third in line is an A-4M. Finally, leading the formation is an AV-8B day attack Harrier II, again assigned to VMAT-203 (*The Boeing Company*)

firepower for US, Korean and Allied forces. Marine Corps aircraft flew from US Navy carriers and bare bones Korean airfields, and in-country sorties came under control of USAF Joint Operations Centers.

In 1948 the Marine Corps had fielded its first helicopters, and these vehicles played an important role in Korea and Vietnam. Helicopters and US Navy light carriers (later amphibious assault ships) formed the cornerstone of the new amphibious assault concept created to meet the challenges of the nuclear battlefield. Following the Korean War, the Marines developed a requirement for a fixed-wing strike aircraft to support helicopter assault operations and to operate from amphibious ships. In 1957, the Marine Commandant, Gen Randolph Pate, sent a letter to the Chief of Naval Operations (CNO) requesting that 'all tactical aircraft have short/vertical take-off and landing capability as soon as is technically feasible without sacrificing existing mission capabilities'.

From 1965 to 1973 Marine aviation deployed more than half of its total force to support ground forces in the Vietnam War. Marine Corps F-4 Phantom IIs, A-4 Skyhawks and F-8 Crusaders provided effective CAS. However, from 1968 Marine fixed-wing sorties in-theatre were concentrated under the control of the USAF. The Marines were less than thrilled with the responsiveness of USAF command centres when it came to generating urgent air power in support of troops in contact (TIC) with the enemy. Combat experience showed that to be effective, air power needed to deliver weapons within 30 minutes of the call coming in if it was to influence the outcome of the battle. The Marine Corps vowed that it would find a way to control its air power in the future so that it could be focused when needed in support of Marine ground operations.

During the Vietnam War, the Marines created a requirement for a new aircraft to eventually replace the much-respected A-4. It would have the basing flexibility of a helicopter and the firepower of a strike aircraft. The only aircraft capable of meeting these requirements was the British Hawker Siddeley Harrier. US Navy, USAF, US Army, RAF and Lufwaffe pilots (but no US Marine Corps pilots) had participated in the 1964-65 tripartite flight evaluation of the Kestrel vertical/short take-off and landing (V/STOL) aircraft – an early version of the Harrier. Marine Corps pilots first flew the Harrier in 1968, and they wrote glowing reports about the capabilities of the jet for the service's CAS mission.

At this time the US Congress debated the best solution for CAS in official hearings. The US Army favoured the AH-56A Cheyenne attack helicopter, the USAF was working the A-X competition which led to the A-10A and the Marine Corps embraced the AV-8A Harrier option – all different and expensive solutions.

Funding for the new Marine Corps AV-8A programme was added to the 1970 defence budget. The Marine Corps agreed to give up three of its F-4 squadrons so as to procure 102 AV-8As and eight TAV-8A two-seat trainers. These aircraft were operated by three tactical squadrons between 1971 and 1990 and a training squadron (from 1975) to develop operational experience with V/STOL aircraft. The rest of the Marine Corps light attack force was filled out with the improved A-4M Skyhawk II, while the reserves flew earlier versions of this aircraft.

Historically, there has always been a healthy friction between the Marine Corps and US Navy over funding of aviation and other programmes since money for the former is included in the budget of the latter. In the past the Marine Corps has followed its own path, separate from the US Navy, on aviation programmes when required – F4U Corsair versus F6F Hellcat fighters in World War 2, AV-8A/A-4M versus A-7 Corsair II light attack aircraft post-Vietnam and the Marine Corps retaining its F-4 Phantom II fighters rather than go to the F-14 Tomcat in the early 1980s while waiting for the F/A-18 Hornet.

Successful operations with the AV-8A Harrier (despite its limited range and payload, high attrition rate and competition for resources with US Navy programmes) convinced senior Marine Corps leadership that they were on the right track toward improved CAS for the service overall. This led to a 1973 requirement for an improved V/STOL attack aircraft to replace the AV-8A and A-4M.

In the late 1970s the Marine Corps and Congress funded the development of the McDonnell Douglas/British Aerospace AV-8B Harrier II, while the DoD, US Navy and elements of Congress battled over whether the F/A-18, AV-8B or even an improved A-4 would be the best solution for the future battlefield. The Marine Corps identified the AV-8B as its number one aviation programme, and despite opposition from the Carter Administration, US Navy and other influential bodies, with support from Congress it eventually won the battle.

The Marine Corps never took the AV-8A Harrier into combat. However, the Royal Navy successfully fought the 1982 Falklands War with its radar-equipped Sea Harrier FRS 1s and the Royal Air Force flew attack missions with its Harrier GR 3s, which were very similar in performance and capability to the AV-8A. This war highlighted the advantages of having a V/STOL tactical aircraft that could fly from medium-sized ships and austere land bases.

In late 1983, the first AV-8B Harrier II day attack aircraft was delivered to Harrier training squadron VMAT-203 at Marine Corps Air Station (MCAS) Cherry Point, North Carolina, to begin transition training for pilots and squadrons. Over the next several years six frontline units transitioned or converted to the day attack AV-8B, VMA-331 transitioning from the A-4M in 1985, VMA-231 transitioning from the AV-8A in 1985, VMA-542 also transitioning from the AV-8A in 1986, VMA-223 transitioning from the A-4M in 1987, VMA-513 transitioning from the AV-8A that same year and VMA-311 transitioning from the A-4M in 1989.

In August 1990, when Iraqi forces invaded Kuwait, the Marine Corps had a single large Harrier II training unit and six operational AV-8B day attack squadrons, each equipped with 20 aircraft. Two new squadrons, VMA-214 and VMA-211, were in the process of transitioning from the A-4M to the AV-8B night attack aircraft, their air- and groundcrews still undertaking intensive training to become familiar with this complex aircraft and its unique mission capabilities.

The Harrier II day attack aircraft remained a single-seat design that was developed to replace both the AV-8A and the A-4. The AV-8B's short take-off and vertical landing capability (STOVL) was provided by the jet's upgraded Rolls-Royce Pegasus F402-RR-406 engine, which produced 21,800 lbs of thrust, via four rotating exhaust nozzles in the central fuselage and reaction controls (jet puffer ducts) located in the nose, tail

and wingtips – the latter controlled aircraft attitude. The Harrier II could operate more efficiently than the AV-8A from amphibious ships, expeditionary airfields, roads and damaged airfields.

The prime missions of the AV-8B were to provide air support for the MAGTF, including performing CAS, deep air support, armed reconnaissance and air interdiction, offensive and defensive anti-air warfare, combat air patrols, armed escort and defence suppression.

Some former Marine Corps A-4 pilots had mixed feelings about transitioning to the AV-8B. Lt Col Cary Branch, XO of VMA-311 during *Desert Storm*, commented on the A-4 versus the AV-8B;

'I had a lot of time flying the A-4 and I had trained on both the two-seater and single-seat F-models. My first tour was on the A-4M at MCAS El Toro, California, with VMA-214. The flying characteristics of one aeroplane versus another were just a matter of preference. The day attack AV-8B, in my opinion, was not any better, except for its V/STOL capability, than an A-4M. You could not even fight it as well in air-to-air combat. I had 3400 hours in the A-4 so I knew it very well.

'What the Harrier II day attack jet did have was modern avionics. One of the biggest differences between the A-4M and Harrier II was the latter's Inertial Navigation System (INS) with a moving map display, which meant we could quickly figure out where we were without having to pull out a map. The jet also had a better Head-Up Display (HUD) and flight controls. And the AV-8B subsequently became an even better combat platform when the night attack systems and higher-thrust (23,500 lbs) Rolls-Royce F402-RR-408 engine were added. When the radar, Forward Looking Infrared (FLIR), laser targeting pod and Joint Direct Attack Munitions (JDAM) came along a decade after we used the aircraft in *Desert Storm*, the Marine Corps had a much better jet. But initially the day attack jet was just a hovering A-4M with an INS, improved controls, displays and better systems.

'We had the Angle Rate Bombing System (ARBS) in the last A-4Ms, but it never worked as well as it did in the Harrier II because the AV-8B's avionics were more modern and reliable. ARBS was a good passive bombing sensor, and it provided a good bombing solution based on optical discrimination of contrast. At times, it could jump lock to a

The first of four full-scale development AV-8Bs (BuNo 161396) leads AV-8C BuNo 159255 during an early test and evaluation sortie from NAS Patuxent River, Maryland, in the early 1980s. BuNo 161396 presently resides in the Naval Test and Evaluation Museum at NAS Pensacola, Florida, while BuNo 159255 was retired by VMA-542 to the Aircraft Maintenance and Regeneration Center at Davis-Monthan AFB, Arizona, in 1987 (*The Boeing Company*)

Right
A close up of the nose of an AV-8B, at the very tip of which is the Hughes ASB-19 Angle Rate Bombing System (ARBS) sensor. Note also the aircraft's large air intakes, refuelling probe and yaw vane, the latter providing jet-borne flight cues to AV-8B pilots (*Peter Mersky collection*)

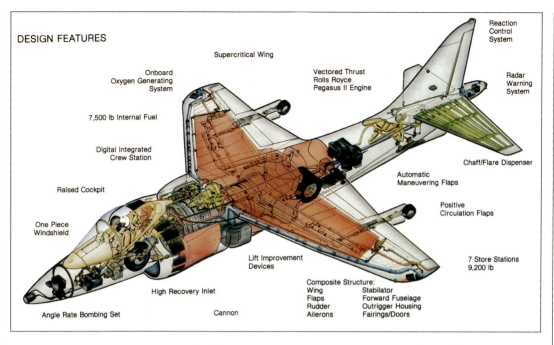

DESIGN FEATURES

Supercritical Wing

Onboard
Oxygen Generating
System

Vectored Thrust
Rolls Royce
Pegasus II Engine

Reaction
Control
System

Radar
Warning
System

7,500 lb Internal Fuel

Digital Integrated
Crew Station

Chaff/Flare Dispenser

Raised Cockpit

Automatic
Maneuvering Flaps

Positive
Circulation Flaps

One Piece
Windshield

Lift Improvement
Devices

7 Store Stations
9,200 lb

High Recovery Inlet

Composite Structure:
Wing   Stabilator
Flaps   Forward Fuselage
Rudder   Outrigger Housing
Ailerons   Fairings/Doors

Angle Rate Bombing Set

Cannon

Above
From the start, the Harrier II programme was an international one involving McDonnell Douglas as prime contractor, British Aerospace as principal subcontractor, Rolls-Royce as engine manufacturer and hundreds of subcontractors in the USA and UK, as well as others in Spain and Italy when those nations decided to procure versions of the AV-8B. The design features listed in this illustration show improvements made in the Harrier II to achieve the goal of doubling the range, payload and capability of the AV-8B over the AV-8A/C (*The Boeing Company*)

brighter contrast just as you were getting ready to release, but a quick switch to the Continuously Computed Impact Point (CCIP) mode worked well. While the A-4M had reached its growth limit the AV-8B was just starting, with better avionics and integration for the pilot.

'Another thing in the Harrier II's favour was the fact that the AV-8Bs we were receiving then were brand new, in contrast to our older A-4s, which were worn out. This meant that you could routinely have 18 or 19 out of 20 jets in a squadron in a full up status.

'I thought the AV-8B was pretty easy to fly. We were able to give them to first-tour aviators. Unlike second-tour guys from AV-8As or A-4s, the new guys did not have any bad habits to overcome from their previous jets. As a former A-4 guy, initially I flew the AV-8B like an A-4, but then started to understand the jet's unique capabilities. Some of my A-4 habits did not translate well, but within a few weeks of training these were gone and I thought the AV-8B was a pretty good aeroplane that was easy to fly. However, V/STOL is a different world, and we crashed quite a few as we had mechanical and technical issues, as well as pilot error. V/STOL was not that hard to "get", but it took more hours to understand, and once you "got it", it became a piece of cake.'

Lt Col Ted Herman began flying the Harrier in 1973, and over the next 19 years had the good fortune to fly the A-4, AV-8A and AV-8B;

'I transitioned to the AV-8A just as the second Harrier squadron

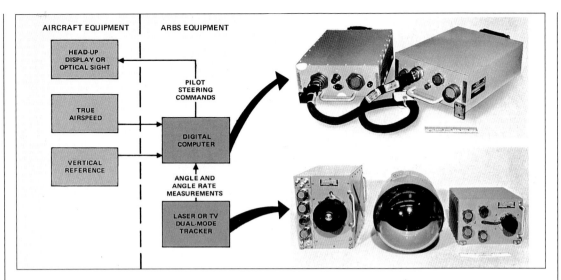

AIRCRAFT EQUIPMENT	ARBS EQUIPMENT

HEAD-UP DISPLAY OR OPTICAL SIGHT

TRUE AIRSPEED

VERTICAL REFERENCE

PILOT STEERING COMMANDS

DIGITAL COMPUTER

ANGLE AND ANGLE RATE MEASUREMENTS

LASER OR TV DUAL-MODE TRACKER

(VMA-542) was forming at MCAS Beaufort, South Carolina. I came to the squadron with about 1200 hours in the EA-6A and the TA-4J. We had no two-seat trainers, simulators or formal training systems at that time. Some of the early pilots were trained in England, but that ended about the time I joined the programme.

'Since our first hop would be solo, we were intensely coached in systems and the use of the throttle and nozzle lever. Our "simulator" was a throttle quadrant attached to a board. We sat at the table and went through our take-off and landing procedures, moving the throttle and nozzle lever appropriately.

'My first two flights were "conventional" take-off and landings. The fully fuelled 16,500-lb jet had 21,800 lbs of thrust that came on within 2.5 seconds of slamming the throttle to full power. The acceleration was awe-inspiring, which blurred the instrument panel and pushed the jet to take-off speed within four seconds or so. By the time a Harrier reached the end of a 10,000-ft USAF runway, it had reached almost 400 knots.

'Another satisfying point about the AV-8A was its extremely light and responsive flight controls – completely different from the relatively heavy stick of the A-4. The AV-8B initially had a heavier flight control feel like the A-4, but it was soon "lightened" following complaints from pilots.

'The A-4M, the last of the Skyhawk line, had a powerful Pratt & Whitney J52-P-408 engine putting out about 11,200 lbs of thrust. That pretty much equated to the Harrier II's F402-RR-406 engine in military power. Side by side, accelerating from 200 knots, the two jets were pretty close in performance. The A-4 cockpit was tiny and cramped compared to the cockpits of both the AV-8A and AV-8B, and the Skyhawk's ejection seat was so narrow that it was like sitting on a stone slab. The Harrier II's Stencel SJ-12 seat reclined slightly, had a cushion and was more comfortable for the pilot. The seat and large cockpit made eight-hour transoceanic flights or multiple sorties per day much less fatiguing, and painful.

'The AV-8B was a different machine when compared to the AV-8A. As a next generation combat aircraft, it was supplied with an extensive ground training system that included simulators, maintenance trainers,

Created by the manufacturer, Hughes, this diagram shows the major components of the ARBS. When the pilot locked this system on a contrast target, ARBS provided bomb delivery information via the HUD. VMFA-542's Col Art Tomassetti told the author that 'the Harrier II cockpit was ideally set up for the attack mission. The ARBS with the TV camera was good, although it did have some limitations that meant it was not the ideal system for all battlefield conditions. When you could lock onto a high contrast target it was very accurate. Indeed, I saw studies that said the AV-8B was a more accurate bomber in these conditions than the F/A-18 Hornet with radar ranging' (*Hughes Aircraft*) a formalised training syllabus and a full-time training squadron. The heavier Harrier II carried 2000 lbs more internal fuel than the AV-8A. It was more versatile in the V/STOL regime, although the jet was not as responsive as the original Harrier. The bigger wing, huge flaps and stronger stability controls system, coupled with an electronically controlled engine, allowed the pilot to carry much more weight into a small field, fly farther and turn harder. The electronic engine control also made shipboard work and confined area operations safer and more predictable.

'The AV-8B's mission computer and INS not only improved bombing solutions, they also gave the pilot extremely accurate navigation and performance calculations. The V/REST (vertical, range, endurance, speed and time) computer allowed the pilot to calculate fuel burn for each leg, on-going "bingos" (fuel states) and highly critical take-off and landing performance. The computer also converted coordinates from latitude/longitude to Universal Transverse Mercator (UTM – a geographic coordinate system that provides a grid-based method of specifying locations on the surface of the Earth) or vice versa. This is a critical capability when performing CAS and talking to FACs who use UTM grids on 1:50K land navigation charts.

'The 25 mm GAU-12 cannon was much more accurate, powerful and reliable, and had a higher cyclic rate (3600 rounds per minute), than the slow-firing 20 mm or 30 mm cannon of the A-4 or the AV-8A, respectively. Accurate strafing in the AV-8B was possible from as high an altitude as 7000 ft in a 30-degree dive, as well as in ten-degree dives. It was like pointing a heat beam at a target. The high cyclic rate made a low-pitched, blender like hum and the heavy recoil caused the nose to rise slightly, which was easily controlled with a bit of forward stick to hold on target.

'Bombing during daylight was easy and the pilot had many options. As he rolled in on the target, he could immediately convert from CCIP to an auto-drop or toss with a simple thumb selection on the stick. Using the ARBS "sweetened" the solution by allowing better pipper placement on the target. The beauty of the ARBS was that it allowed pilots to use the systems that suited them best, resulting in extremely fine accuracy. Its targeting system was in fact more accurate than the design CEP (circular error probable) of the weapon being employed.'

The AV-8B was designed to accommodate a wide range of weapons, including (from front to back) AIM-9 Sidewinder missiles (row one), SUU-44 flare dispensers (row two), LAU-68/61/10 2.75- and 5-inch rocket pods (rows three and four), Mk 77 napalm canisters (row five), Mk 20 Rockeye II CBUs (row six), Mk 81 250-lb bombs (row seven), Mk 82 500-lb bombs (row eight), Mk 83 1000-lb bombs (row nine) and triple ejector weapons racks. Not shown is the GAU-12 25 mm cannon and 300 rounds of ammunition mounted in two pods beneath the fuselage of the AV-8B (*The Boeing Company*)

VMA-311 AND MAG-13 (FORWARD)

At the end of the Iran-Iraq War (1980-88), Iraq was bankrupt and several of its cities and much of its infrastructure near the border with Iran were in ruins. Iraqi dictator Saddam Hussein showed no interest in paying back war debts to his Middle Eastern neighbours who had funded the long-running conflict. He even threatened to attack one of his key creditors, oil-rich Kuwait (a country that Iraq refused to officially recognise following its creation in 1961 – it had previously been a British dependency), unless his demands for debt relief on the $5.5 billion that was owed to the Sheikdom were not met. Saddam made good on his threat at 0200 hrs on 2 August 1990 when more than 120,000 troops and 300 tanks of the Iraqi Republican Guard (IRG) crossed the border and advanced rapidly into Kuwait.

The invasion caught most of the country's 30,000-man military by surprise because the Emir of Kuwait, Sheikh Jaber Ahmed al-Sabah, had lowered the alert status in an attempt to give Saddam no cause to attack. The first warning of an invasion came around midnight on 1/2 August when balloon-borne radars identified the approach of numerous vehicles from the north. Kuwaiti air and ground forces fought back, allowing the Emir and his family to escape to Saudi Arabia.

By 3 August Iraqi forces had taken up positions in much of Kuwait, and they began preparing defensive fortifications. That same day Saddam announced that Kuwait had become Iraq's 19th province, and his troops set about fortifying the Kuwait-Saudi border. In late August IRG forces pulled back to positions in southern Iraq after they were replaced by ten divisions (about 150,000 troops) of the regular army.

When the IRG seized Kuwait, they also took control of a quarter of the world's oil supply. Despite this, there was no significant military action undertaken by nearby countries to stop Iraq from moving further south. The Gulf Cooperative Council (GCC), made up of Saudi Arabia, Kuwait, Bahrain, Qatar, the United Arab Emirates and the Sultanate of

Lt Col Dick White, CO of VMA-311, poses in front of one of his newly repainted AV-8Bs at MCAS Cherry Point just prior to departing for the Middle East. This photograph shows the aircraft in ferry configuration, with single AIM-9Ms on the outer launch pylons, 300 US gallon external fuel tanks on each of the inner pylons and the two pods for the 25 mm GAU-12 cannon on the centreline (*Dick White*)

AV-8Bs of VMA-311 line up at MCAS Cherry Point, ready for their departure to the Middle East. The 'Tomcats' became the first Harrier II unit committed to *Desert Shield*, since it had been training for a deployment to Japan. The squadron left its home base of MCAS Yuma on 15 August 1990 and flew to MCAS Cherry Point, North Carolina, where its jets were repainted with a 'grey-on-grey' camouflage scheme that was more appropriate for the Middle East environment

VMA-311's 'Cat 04' (BuNo 163660) looks resplendent in its recently applied 'grey-on-grey' camouflage scheme, this photograph having been taken soon after the jet was repainted (*Dick White*)

Oman, rushed military units to positions along the Saudi-Kuwait border, but these small forces would not have been able to stop any large Iraqi attack.

On 2 August US President George H W Bush signed an executive order declaring a national emergency. He also ordered US Central Command (CENTCOM) to prepare for the defence of Saudi Arabia and other nations in the region, and to initiate planning to drive Iraqi units out of Kuwait. That same day the United Nations' Security Council passed Resolution 660, which condemned the invasion and called for an immediate Iraqi withdrawal. On 6 August Saudi King Fahad met with US Secretary of Defense Richard B 'Dick' Cheney and CENTCOM Commander-in-Chief Gen Norman Schwarzkopf and invited the USA and other nations to send military forces to the Kingdom. In the past, Saudi Arabia had not allowed foreign troops to be based on its soil unless the country was faced with a serious emergency.

In reaction to the Iraqi invasion of Kuwait, 'Dick' Cheney ordered Gen Colin L Powell, Chairman of the Joint Chiefs of Staff, to activate a massive US force and quickly move it to the Middle East in support of Operation *Desert Shield* in an effort to stall further Iraqi aggression. The Marine Corps was a vital part of this effort, and forces ashore were assigned to US Marine Forces Central Command, led by Lt Gen Walter E Boomer, while Marine Forces Afloat came under the command of Vice Adm Henry H Mauz Jr, US Naval Forces Central Command.

On 7 August USAF fighters began arriving at airfields in Saudi Arabia, along with transport aircraft carrying elements of the US Army's 82nd Airborne Division. Units of the Marine Corps' 7th Marine Expeditionary Brigade (MEB) from California – the lead element of 1st Marine Expeditionary Force (I MEF) – were airlifted to Saudi Arabia in late August, followed a short while later by 1st MEB from Hawaii. On landing, Marine Corps forces met up with Maritime Prepositioning Ships (MPSs) loaded with equipment that had docked at the port of Al Jubail in Saudi Arabia.

Marine Corps units then assumed defensive positions along the border, starting on 25 August 1990. For the first half of *Desert Shield*,

Marine Corps units made up about half of the US ground forces in defensive positions and a quarter of the aircraft.

The deployment of air power into the region was rapid. Within a week there were more than 300 Allied aircraft on the ground, and within a month 1200+ had arrived. One of the Coalition challenges was to find air bases for the arriving aircraft. Amongst the first US units to deploy to the region were elements of 3rd Marine Aircraft Wing (MAW), led by Maj Gen (later Lt Gen) Royal N Moore. This was the air combat element sent to support I MEF, and squadrons assigned to it were equipped with A-6E Intruders, F/A-18A/C/D Hornets and AV-8B Harrier IIs. The latter were flown by VMA-311 'Tomcats' from MCAS Yuma, Arizona, and VMA-542 'Tigers' from MCAS Cherry Point.

VMA-311 can trace its combat history back to late 1942 flying F4U Corsairs in the Pacific in World War 2, followed by F9F Panthers over Korea and A-4 Skyhawks in Vietnam. In March 1989 the unit began its transition from the A-4M to the AV-8B, becoming the last Marine Corps light attack squadron to convert to the day attack variant of the Harrier II. Now retired, Col Dick White, who (as a lieutenant colonel) was the CO of the 'Tomcats' at the time, recalled;

'We left Yuma on 15 August and went to Cherry Point, where our aircraft were repainted and final maintenance completed. At about 2200 hrs on the 18th we left Cherry Point for a night flight across the Atlantic to Rota, Spain. As you can imagine, we had some pretty tight gentlemen in the cockpits of those jets, as half of my pilots had never

This map of the Middle East shows the geography of Operations Desert Shield and Desert Storm, as well as the operating locations of Marine Corps Harrier II units during the conflict. The AV-8Bs would fly 5973 sorties totalling 7080 hours between 15 August 1990 and 16 January 1991 as part of Desert Shield (US Marine Corps)

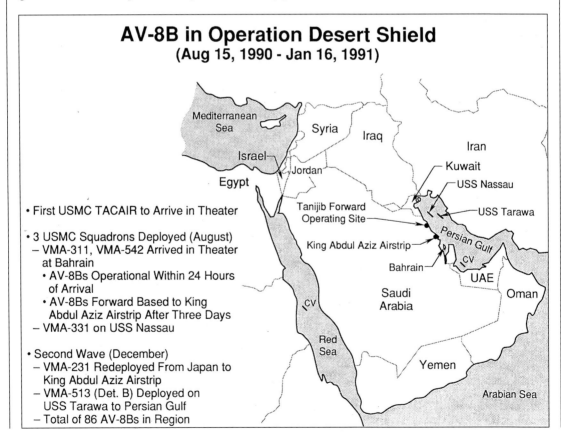

AV-8B in Operation Desert Shield
(Aug 15, 1990 - Jan 16, 1991)

- First USMC TACAIR to Arrive in Theater

- 3 USMC Squadrons Deployed (August)
  - VMA-311, VMA-542 Arrived in Theater at Bahrain
    - AV-8Bs Operational Within 24 Hours of Arrival
    - AV-8Bs Forward Based to King Abdul Aziz Airstrip After Three Days
  - VMA-331 on USS Nassau

- Second Wave (December)
  - VMA-231 Redeployed From Japan to King Abdul Aziz Airstrip
  - VMA-513 (Det. B) Deployed on USS Tarawa to Persian Gulf
  - Total of 86 AV-8Bs in Region

Mediterranean Sea
Syria
Iraq
Iran
Israel
Jordan
Kuwait
USS Nassau
Egypt
USS Tarawa
Tanijib Forward Operating Site
Persian Gulf
King Abdul Aziz Airstrip
Bahrain
CV
UAE
Saudi Arabia
Oman
CV
Red Sea
Yemen
Arabian Sea

tanked at night, half had never tanked off a KC-10 and none had done both! It was an exciting crossing, with storms and 11 refuellings. From Rota we flew on to Bahrain.'

Lt Col Cary Branch, also now retired, served (with the rank of major) as the executive officer of VMA-311 in 1990;

'We were preparing for a deployment to MCAS Iwakuni, Japan, when Saddam's forces went into Kuwait. I did not even know where Kuwait was, yet two-and-a-half weeks later we were sitting strip alert in the desert of Saudi Arabia! The whole thing came as quite a surprise to both us and our families! I am pretty sure that is why we went first, as we were ready to go to Japan. We had already done all the planning and packing, and we were a fully stabilised squadron, while other units were still in the process of transitioning.

'Our flight to Cherry Point from Yuma was supported by Marine Corps KC-130s. With only a few days in Cherry Point to prepare, the base personnel were going crazy as they were not only getting our squadron ready, but also others equipped with AV-8Bs and A-6Es. We flew in with grey and green jets that were horrible for the desert, as they looked like dark green dots. So we lined them up, taped them up and spray-painted them with water-based paints to make them desert camouflage compatible. NADEP (Naval Aviation Depot) then took over and we worked as a team. Jets were getting painted rapidly and stuff packed, as we had to be ready for our tanker time. If we missed the tanker support window, we would have lost our slot, and who knew when we would have had another opportunity to go?

'The flight to Rota was a challenge, seeing that none of us have ever tanked off KC-10s. We took off in a storm and the weather was dark and nasty. We met up with a tanker about 300 miles offshore over the Atlantic. I led five aeroplanes, and we had four groups of five jets going across. I remember seeing the tanker in the dark, and it reminded me of the movie *Close Encounters of the Third Kind*. The KC-10 had massive lights, and it was huge compared to the KC-130s we usually refuelled from. When I came up I asked, "Can you dim half of those lights?" We all tanked, and by the time we neared Rota we had refuelled so many times that we had become comfortable with doing so.'

At the end of August 1990 the Marine Corps decided to focus AV-8B operations at King Abdul Aziz Naval Base, on the northern coast of Saudi Arabia. VMA-311 moved from Sheikh Isa Air Base in Bahrain to this austere facility so as to provide direct support for Marine Corps units on the ground holding the defensive line along the Saudi-Kuwait

AV-8Bs of VMA-311 refuel from a USAF KC-10 tanker en route to Bahrain. The Harrier II could only tank via probe and drogue refuelling systems, and in 1990 most of the USAF tankers were KC-135s equipped with the boom refuelling system. The latter could be fitted with a drogue kit, but the resulting modification did not work well with the AV-8B's short, folding refuelling probe. Fortunately, the USAF's KC-10 tankers were fitted with both the 'flying boom' and probe and drogue refuelling systems, which made the aircraft suitable for supporting AV-8B units heading for the Middle East. The flight from MCAS Cherry Point to NAS Rota, Spain, was a challenge as the weather was poor en route, much of the flight took place at night and only a handful of the VMA-311 pilots had ever tanked from a KC-10. Up to a dozen refuelling connections had to be made during the ferry flight so as to ensure that the Harrier II pilots had sufficient fuel to make it to divert airfields along the route in the event of a weather or systems problem (*Dick White*)

border. Lt Col Dick White commented on this move;

'After a few days in Bahrain we went to King Abdul Aziz, a small airstrip within a Saudi naval base on the Arabian Gulf. The strip was in poor shape, but it had facilities, including a soccer stadium, nearby. For the next 60 days we had four aircraft armed with bombs and manned by pilots ready on strip alert just in case the Iraqi army did something.

'We were the first Harrier II squadron to deploy to *Desert Shield*, arriving in-theatre with the 82nd Airborne Division. At 60 days there were enough other jets in the region – Hornets, Intruders and USAF types – to help us with the alert. However, we did maintain four jets at the ready as we were the closest to the border, and could be called to go at any time. Indeed, we received a lot of attention because we were so close to the Kuwait border. We were right behind the 82nd Airborne and elements of the 1st Marine Division (MARDIV), who were in a blocking position should Saddam's forces come down the coastal highway.

'Gen Boomer, the three star I MEF commander, came down to visit VMA-311 just 24 hours after we arrived. I escorted him around and showed him that we had sufficient aircraft and ordnance, which was all we needed to fly strikes. I told him we could be overhead in five minutes after the call. Gen Boomer walked around petting the Harrier IIs like a farmer petting his favourite horses. He was glad to see those jets, let me tell you.

'We got a lot of visitors and were asked a lot of questions from the media, as we were the only Marine squadron in Saudi Arabia for 60 days. We were the closest to the battle zone, and thus the media wanted to come and talk to the idiots that were where the fight might start. Reporters asked why we were this close to the border. We told them that the Marines and other troops were on the ground up there and the Harrier II was the dedicated Marine CAS aircraft. We were not 300 miles in the rear at Riyadh like a lot of the USAF squadrons. We were here so that we could be over the heads of the Marines in five minutes if we got the call for support.'

Being near the port of Al Jubail, with US Navy supply and repair ships close by, and ready access to fuel, ordnance, spare parts and supplies, King Abdul Aziz proved the ideal location for supporting AV-8B operations.

Lt Col Cary Branch gave the following account of the base move;

'It was bizarre to go from Sheik Isa to King Abdul Aziz, where we set up a strip alert to be ready just in case the Iraqis moved south. We went from a nice place in Bahrain to a site just down the freeway from the Saudi-Kuwait border along the coast. When we landed here there was nothing. We had a beat up asphalt strip, a soccer stadium and almost no shelter. The maintenance people started working out of boxes, and there was no hangar space.

'We got everything Marine Corps units would need to deploy quickly from the MPSs. This was just as well, for we didn't even have tents at first. We simply had our sleeping bags, which we rolled out on the ground and slept in the open. We did have fuel bladders, water and ordnance – including Mk 82s and Mk 20 Rockeye IIs – and this allowed us to have ten jets ready to go at various alert levels from 15 minutes to an hour or so. The guys on strip alert sat around with their gear on in 110-degree heat with 90 percent

An aerial view of King Abdul Aziz Naval Base in Saudi Arabia. The facility's single short runway can clearly be seen, as can the flightline and the soccer stadium in the upper right corner of the shot. The facility's close proximity to the Arabian Gulf and a major highway made it the ideal location from a logistical standpoint, but these features also meant that defending the base in the event of an attack would be more of a challenge. Personnel from the AV-8B squadrons and co-located maintenance units were responsible for protecting the airfield against ground attack from land or sea. Fortifications were also set up to protect critical facilities and personnel from air or Scud missile attacks, with Improved HAWK and Stinger SAM batteries located nearby (*Ted Herman*)

Marine Corps armourers prepare Mk 82 500-lb bombs at King Abdul Aziz Naval Base shortly after VMA-311's arrival in Saudi Arabia. The logistics support and rearming requirements of an AV-8B squadron and co-located VMO-1 and -2 (equipped with OV-10s) was quite heavy once *Desert Storm* commenced. These units received assistance from Marine Wing Support Squadron 174 and MALS-13, as well as the US Navy Seabees, when it came to creating facilities and maintenance and logistics networks. In addition, a number of Maritime Prepositioning Ships and US Navy support vessels docked at the nearby port of Al Jubail to deliver ordnance, squadron support kits and other critical materials (*Dick White*)

humidity – crappy weather. But that is what Marines did.

'Things soon improved, as we took over the soccer field, which was brand new and had never been used. Although the stadium was covered in sand, it had showers and real toilets. We put up tents in the stadium and made offices. We even had to set up our own perimeter security. We were close to the highway and only a mile-and-a-half from the water.

'Within weeks of our arrival at King Abdul Aziz we could tell that the defensive line just north of us at the border between Kuwait and Saudi Arabia was working. Things got better from that point onwards, as we settled into the soccer stadium, set up hard-back tents and dug fortifications. More Marines also continued to arrive, including a Hawk (air defence) battery that set up on a hill near the stadium'

By mid-September 1990 the Coalition had, either on the ground or in transit, sufficient land, air and sea forces to stop any Iraqi thrust into Saudi Arabia. Leaders then focused on plans to build up the larger assault forces needed to retake Kuwait. Allied ground assets in position included troops from the Royal Saudi Land Forces, Saudi National Guard, Bahrain, Oman, Qatar, United Arab Emirates, Egypt, Syria, Great Britain, France and the US Army and Marine Corps. Most of these forces were located along the border between Saudi Arabia and Kuwait, running from Dhahran in the southeast to King Khalid City in the west.

The US Navy and Marine Corps sent all available amphibious forces that could be mustered to the Near East region, including the 4th MEB, 13th MEU (SOC) and MAGTF 6-90. They in turn forced the Iraqis to create elaborate beach defences along the Kuwait and Iraqi coasts to deal with potential amphibious landings. Included in this large fleet of more than 30 ships was USS *Nassau* (LHA-4), which had VMA-331 and its 20 AV-8Bs embarked. More than 50 Allied naval vessels, including three US aircraft carrier battlegroups, patrolled the Arabian Sea.

Col John Bioty Jr was given the job of commanding MAG-13 (Forward). This unit, based at King Abdul Aziz, eventually controlled more than 3000 Marines, three and one-third squadrons of AV-8Bs, two squadrons (VMO-1 and -2) of OV-10 surveillance aircraft and support and air defence forces. Now-retired Col Bioty told the author;

'Lt Gen Harold Blott, Assistant Wing Commander of 3rd MAW and a former AV-8A pilot, called me in mid-August and asked, "What are you doing? We are moving Harrier IIs from Bahrain to Saudi Arabia and I need a colonel to lead MAG-13 (Forward)". I was Deputy Director of the Marine Command and Staff Course at Marine Corps Base Quantico, Virginia, at that time, so I grabbed my flight gear and went back to VMAT-203 – the AV-8B training squadron – in early September 1990 to refresh my Harrier II qualifications. Here, I was given a short, ten-hour syllabus to work through as it had only been three months since I had been flying as CO of an AV-8B squadron. Things came back quickly, as I had 3500 hours of flying in my logbook, at least 2000 of which were in Harriers.

'I took the "big bird" over to the Middle East on 16 September 1990, landing in Bahrain. Having spent a few days talking with Col John Dempsey from MAG-32 while at Cherry Point, I then met with Maj Gen Royal Moore to be briefed on his desires for MAG-13 (Forward).

'At that time we had one squadron, VMA-311, at King Abdul Aziz Naval Base, and I was to go up there to get stuff organised and lend senior credibility to that forward-deployed site. I got to King Abdul Aziz, saw what we had there and then oversaw the construction of a facility to handle more units. I also started flying right away just to get a feel for the area, and situation. Everything looked like a sand bowl. The process of building the base up was a pleasure, for I had Lt Col Jim Chesom, CO of the Marine Wing Support Squadron 174 out of Japan, running things. He and his personnel built aircraft sites and fuel pits and ran other critical support services.

'At King Abdul Aziz I met with Adm Badr from the Saudi Navy, and he told me that the naval base was to have been the facility that supported a Saudi naval academy at Al Jubail, but there had been a problem with the building contractors. A significant part of the base had been completed, but this had been left unoccupied, and since liberally covered with sand, as the project was never totally finished. It had a large soccer stadium with an Astroturf field, running water in most buildings, many of which were air conditioned, and a single asphalt runway suitable for light civil aircraft with low pressure tyres or executive jet operations. Overall, it was a super facility for us.

'I developed a small staff including a few officers from VMA-311. Lt Col Dick White, CO of VMA-331, and I had known each other for a long time, and we worked well together. We started to beg, borrow and steal stuff in an effort to expand the base in preparation for a possible war, and to add other units and create a wing staff. You talk about knee-knocking times, in late September and into October 1990 we still had the daily threat of an Iraqi attack into Saudi Arabia from Kuwait, as there were 500,000 Iraqi troops massed along the border.

'My command was given the title MAG-13 (Forward) after MAG-70 – the first air group deployed to the Gulf – became too large an organisation to be run effectively. It was subsequently broken up into MAG-11 with F/A-18s and MAG-13 with AV-8Bs and OV-10s. Eventually, MAG-13 controlled a total of 86 aircraft (66 Harrier IIs and 20 OV-10s) at King Abdul Aziz.

'Soon after I reached Saudi Arabia, Maj Gen Moore told me to prepare for the arrival of a second squadron of AV-8Bs, and we started making room for them at King Abdul Aziz. Ted Herman was CO of VMA-542, and we had known each other a long time. He was in Bahrain as a part of MAG-70 when I arrived in-theatre, and he led VMA-542 once the unit flew into Sheikh Isa in late August. On 5 November VMA-542 was transferred to King Abdul Aziz and came under the control of MAG-13. This doubled our air strength to 40 jets, and added 250 additional troops.

'Throughout *Desert Shield* we remained in a totally defensive posture, our primary mission being to delay any effort by the Iraqis to move south.

We would have cycled aircraft and bombed the Iraqis around the clock if they had moved against our forces. Our job was also to supply I MEF and Coalition forces with CAS. From 22 August until Thanksgiving, our primary focus was defence, and it remained this way until the end of Exercise *Imminent Thunder* (a highly publicised amphibious exercise along the eastern Saudi Arabian coast, which acted as a final rehearsal of CENTCOM's defensive plans) on 21 November, when we started to begin thinking offensively.

'We had a close working relationship with Maj Gen J M Myatt's I MEF, which sent its FACs down to us at an early stage so as to get them involved with our air operations. With Maj Gen Moore's support, we worked closely with both the Marine division and the pan Arab forces up north to coordinate our CAS.'

Planning for the air campaign against Iraqi forces was commenced as early as 3 August 1990 by the USAF component of US Central Command Air Forces (CENTAF). By month-end a detailed air attack plan (which included involvement by all US services), entitled *Instant Thunder*, was being briefed to the US Joint Chiefs of Staff. In September, Royal Air Force staff officers were asked to participate and, later, representatives from the Royal Saudi Air Force and other Coalition air arms joined the team.

The plan called for a four-phase offensive air campaign. Phase I was a strategic campaign against Iraq. Phase II focused on destroying Iraqi air defences in the Kuwait theatre of operations (KTO). Phase III's goal was the neutralisation of the Iraqi Army and Republican Guard forces and isolation of the KTO. Phase IV was support for the ground offensive to force Iraqi units out of Kuwait. The plan was later changed so that Phases I through III could take place simultaneously over an 18-day period, depending upon the weather.

Once the overall plan was approved, a daily Air Tasking Order (ATO) for every Allied air unit was created. This was a two-part, 200-page, document, the first part of which provided daily sortie assignments while the second section detailed communications frequencies and the assignment of all support missions such as tankers and suppression of enemy air defenses (SEAD).

Gen Charles Horner, C-in-C CENTAF, had a good working relationship with Maj Gen Moore, and early on they struck a deal that if all of the A-6E, EA-6B and half of the F/A-18 sorties were committed to the joint air effort, the Marine Corps would have full control of its other air assets, including AV-8Bs, OV-10s, KC-130s and C-12s. While the US Joint Air Command and Control would direct all air assets, over I MEF's operational area the Marine Corps would control direct air support and tactical air defence operations at lower altitudes.

With political efforts having failed to persuade Saddam to pull his troops out of Iraq, combat now seemed inevitable. On 6 November President Bush called for a substantial increase in American and Coalition forces in the region. Soon, some 100 ships carrying additional ground and air units, supplies and support systems were rerouted to the region or returning to the USA for additional supplies. This included the deployment of several heavy armoured divisions from Europe, a second Marine Corps division from the USA and additional air and naval forces.

The US Navy sent Amphibious Group 3, with 5th MEB embarked, to bolster Marine Corps forces in the region in November.

By January 1991, the US Navy/Marine Corps had assembled the largest amphibious assault force in the Arabian Gulf and Indian Ocean since the Inchon landings during the Korean War. Arab and European contingents also deployed additional ground and air units. Eventually, the Coalition fielded 600,000 troops, 2300 tanks, 1500 helicopters and 150 naval vessels.

The overall operational plan for an air assault on Iraqi forces in Kuwait was designed to disrupt the military capabilities of troops entrenched along the country's border with Saudi Arabia, thus isolating them from their command and control structure in Iraq. This plan called for Coalition air power to bomb Iraqi infrastructure and air defences, rapidly achieve air superiority and reduce by half or more the effectiveness of Iraqi ground forces in and around Kuwait through continuous air attacks. Once this was accomplished a Coalition ground invasion force could attack and drive Iraqi forces from Kuwait with maximum speed and minimum casualties.

Iraqi forces in and around Kuwait were not sitting ducks, however. Indeed, many of the 545,000 troops in the KTO and southern Iraq were battle-hardened from years of conflict with Iran. In the main well equipped with armour, artillery and air defences, they also held the advantage of defensive fortifications that included minefields, fire trenches and mutual supporting firepower. Iraq had also used chemical munitions against both the Iranians and the Kurds during the Iran-Iraq War. One of the Coalition's major fears was becoming bogged down trying to penetrate Iraqi fortifications during the ground offensive and then coming under attack by artillery and chemical munitions.

During preparations for the support of the ground offensive, CENTAF was wary of the Iraqi Air Force (IrAF) targeting Coalition airfields such as King Abdul Aziz, as Lt Col Cary Branch recalled;

'When we initially commenced training flights for the coming offensive, we were restricted from flying above 8000 ft, as that was an engagement zone in case the IrAF attacked. They had a good-sized air arm, and they could have come down and bombed our bases. They *could*

A VMA-311 AV-8B with AGM-65E Laser Mavericks about to be loaded. This precision-guided missile has a 300-lb penetrating warhead, which is very effective. However, the weapon requires laser illumination by a FAC on the ground or in the air for effective targeting, and the day attack Harrier II had no self-designating capability at this early stage in its operational career. Col Art Tomasetti of VMA-542 told the author, 'We did carry Laser Maverick, but only infrequently. I personally gave them a tour of the battlespace on a few occasions, but never fired one principally because I had no laser designator available to me.' During the ground war phase Harrier II pilots expended a total of 36 AGM-65Es, the weapon often featuring in a mixed load of two 'LMAVs' and two to four Mk 82s or Mk 20s so as to cover multiple attack options (*Dick White*)

King Abdul Aziz Naval Base

Jubail, Saudi Arabia (*N 26 55 57, E 049 42 50*)
Runway 15/33, 7,900 Ft. x 148' Ft., Elevation: *32* Ft.

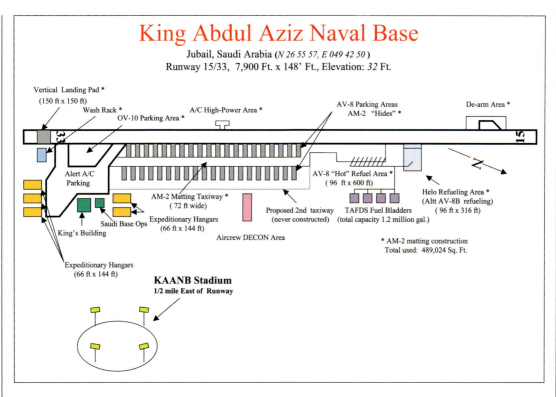

have, but they didn't, and we were ready for them. Our air-to-air guys (USAF F-15s and Marine Corps F/A-18s) were flying CAPs above us, so we had to stay below 8000 ft or risk being shot at by our fighters or Hawk and Patriot SAM batteries.

'We therefore had little choice but to take-off and fly around in the dust and sand at lower altitudes, trying to get the lay of the land without actually being able to see very much. We flew from point to point using our INS and visual landmarks. The sky was brown, the ground was brown and there was blowing dust all of the time. Visibility was often three miles or less. You would fly around and look down and see an oasis. It looked like 1000 years ago, with camels and tents. It was bizarre, like you had gone back in time.

'We flew the jets and exercised the crews, keeping them fully mission-capable and ready for action. Things started settling in, supply was getting better and the living conditions and maintenance facilities also improved. Col Bioty brought in his leadership and tied things together.

'We were fully mission ready by October, as the weather had steadily improved to the point where you could clearly see the ground on virtually every sortie. By November we wanted to get started and then be home by Christmas. That month we also began dropping more bombs on nearby ranges, working out potential kill boxes in Kuwait and developing a plan of action through the ATO with the USAF. We got the Marine Corps Direct Air Support Center (DASC) established so that it could provide us with command and control when it came to getting to and from the battle zone, as well as helping us conduct offensive CAS for friendly units. As winter approached we were confident, and having been in-theatre since August we wanted to get the war started and done.

'Since we were the first unit there, VMA-311 settled in and did the groundwork for the units that followed. We duly supported VMA-542 when it joined us in November, showing pilots the terrain, tactics and operational plans. We were all Harrier II guys, and we knew each other from training command and VMAT-203. VMA-542 then provided the same mentoring role for VMA-231 when it arrived in late December.

'Our primary job by then was to get everyone ready for war. We routinely flew two-jet section training flights near the border and over significant terrain features until we were all ready to operate as a team.'

By December 1990, VMA-311 consisted of 20 officers, 203 enlisted Marines, three enlisted and two officer-level US Navy personnel and two civilian technical representatives. This team maintained a phenomenal full mission capable rate of 90.5 percent during the month, with its complement of 20 aircraft flying 365 training sorties.

Following President Bush's speech in November, the Harrier II units in-theatre realised that they would soon be joined by additional air assets, as Col John Bioty Jr explained to the author;

'I knew all of the Harrier II squadron commanders, and I got to know the COs of the OV-10 units in Saudi too. VMA-231's CO, Lt Col "Rusty" Jones, had been a friend of mine for many years, and he led his unit out to Saudi Arabia in late December 1990. I was the former CO of VMA-331 – the first AV-8B unit – and knew its current boss, Lt Col Jerry Fitzgerald, well. He and his squadron embarked on *Nassau* in mid-August 1990 and sailed for the Middle East.

'The Marine Corps wanted to maintain the flexibility of having the Harrier IIs on the assault ships knowing full well that they might want to make an amphibious type landing somewhere along the Kuwaiti coast. Wanting that support, I do not blame them for not sending VMA-331 ashore once LHA-4 was in-theatre.

'By that time the President had delivered his ultimatum and things were pretty tense. We knew war was near and another Harrier II squadron was coming, and we had had time to erect tents for the troops and add more parking areas and support facilities so that we were prepared to receive the new unit. The last Harrier II squadron to arrive at King Abdul Aziz was Detachment Bravo of VMA-513. The unit had been aboard *Tarawa* as a part of 5th MEF. There were high-level discussions about whether or not they were going to come ashore, and eventually the Det arrived on 15 February 1991 and fought the war alongside us. So that was my full team. Det Bravo brought MAG-13's Harrier II force up to 66 jets. There were another 19 AV-8Bs on *Nassau*.

'I cannot say enough about the Seabees and Marine Wing Support Squadrons who worked with us, as they were worth their weight in gold. They built up a turnaround strip at Tanajib, 35 miles south of the Iraqi border, for rearming and refuelling using a narrow runway and AM-2 aluminium matting for turnaround areas. This facility was secured following negotiations with the Saudi government, the forward operating site having previously been used by small helicopters owned by the Arab-American Oil Company. Its parking and turnaround ramp was expanded using AM-2 matting, and it was stocked with fuel, ordnance and other essentials to allow for rapid refuelling and rearming of AV-8Bs to enable higher sortie rates to be achieved.

'For distances, from King Abdul Aziz it was about 90 nautical miles to the border, 60 nautical miles to Bahrain and a similar distance east to the Iranian flight exclusion region, which ran down the middle of the Arabian Gulf. Tanajib was just 35 nautical miles from the border.'

The desert terrain favoured effective application of air power and speed of advance with armoured forces. Initially, the primary mission of the AV-8B units assigned to MAG-13 and afloat was to support Marine Corps and Coalition forces in the event of an attack by Iraqi forces, bombing them in Kuwait to prepare the battlefield for the Coalition assault (Phase III of the air campaign). The jets would then provide CAS for the Coalition advance into the KTO (Phase IV of the air campaign).

'Ten days before the war started Maj Gen Moore called us together', Col Bioty continued. 'He had moved his 3rd MAW HQ from Bahrain to Jubail Naval Base just west of the port. He got us in a room protected by a guard and told us "At 0300 hrs on 17 January 1991 the attack on Baghdad will begin. Are you ready to go to war?" We knew there was an ultimatum on the table with Saddam Hussein and something had to give.

'In my heart of hearts, until Christmas time, I thought we might find a way not to go to war. Vice President Dan Quayle had visited us on 31 December. We had an hour of time together, and he told me President Bush was very intent on getting the Kuwait situation over and done with so that our troops could be sent back home. He would not confirm anything. I became convinced that either Saddam was going to pull back soon or we would go after him.

'We went offensive on 17 January 1991, with CAS in support of I MEF and the Coalition being our basic mission. Prior to that, however, battlefield shaping and preparing Kuwait for liberation by the Coalition took priority. There was a prepared D-Day ATO, at the heart of which was the planned sanitisation of the battlefield for medium and high altitude operations. We planned to fly at 22,000-24,000 ft and dive down to deliver our weapons. We started flying practice missions well before the start of the air war. We also had officers assigned to help develop the ATO.

'From the start we planned to keep the Harrier IIs ready to support ground forces. A few days before 17 January, Maj Gen Moore visited and he told the pilots we were going to war soon. We tried to keep this quiet from the troops. Gen Boomer was also a regular visitor prewar, while I went to HQ as often as I could to attend senior briefings. Gens Boomer and Horner had a great relationship throughout this period, Horner famously telling the I MEF boss, "Walt, I am glad you are here. I do not want your aeroplanes. I just want your help".'

By January 1991 time had run out for Iraq. On the 12th the US Congress authorised the use of force to remove Iraqi forces from Kuwait. Three days later the UN deadline for Iraq to withdraw its troops from Kuwait passed. By then the Coalition had secured an accurate assessment of Iraqi defences.

Phase I air attacks began on the night of 17 January and continued until the end of the war on 28 February. Initially, many precision strike assets were redirected in support of the effort to find and destroy mobile Scud ballistic missile launchers after Iraq started firing these weapons at Israel and Saudi Arabia. Other tactical jets such as USAF F-111s,

F-15Es, F-16s and A-10s, US Navy and Marine Corps F/A-18s, A-6s, A-7s and AV-8Bs and Coalition A-4s, Tornado Gr 1s, Mirage F 1s and Jaguars concentrated on Phases II and III of the air campaign, attacking Iraqi forces in Kuwait and southern Iraq to pave the way for the ground offensive.

'On the morning of 17 January we had a lot of Harrier II pilots and troops cheering as jets were going overhead into Iraq', Col Bioty recalled. 'We were given 60 targets ourselves to hit in pre-planned strikes during the first day of the war – rocket batteries, long-range artillery and anything that could reach out to hit the 1st and 2nd Marine Divisions and Coalition forces. The Marines had moved forward closer to the border just before the start of the air war. These pre-planned missions were cancelled, however, as there were not enough electronic warfare (EW) assets available to knock out all of the SAMs and AAA radars in the KTO. Maj Gen Moore did not want any aircraft – Harrier II, Hornet or Intruder – to fly unless it had the appropriate escort and jamming support. All of MAG-11's EA-6B EW assets were committed to the deep strike attacks.

'Maj Gen Moore kept 50 percent of the Hornets assigned to the "air-to-mud" mission in Kuwait. MAG-11 had provided the northern CAP throughout *Desert Shield*, but the US Navy took over this mission for *Desert Storm* so that we could focus on supporting ground forces.

'There was a lot of disappointment when the Day One missions were scrubbed, as I had had each squadron commander come and brief me on their 20 assigned targets and how they were going to attack them. And I know we had a pretty good game plan to knock out the FROGs (Free Rocket Over Ground – a family of Soviet-designed short-range battlefield support rockets used by the Iraqis) and artillery within the area of southern Kuwait below Al Jaber.'

Although the preplanned strikes had been scrubbed, VMA-311's alert division nevertheless gave the AV-8B its combat debut on the morning of 17 January, as Lt Col Cary Branch explained;

'I just happened to be the VMA-311 alert division flight lead – it was pure chance that I was on duty. We got the word that Iraqi artillery was firing on Khafji – LAUNCH! Of course the Harrier IIs were ready. I get goose pimples even now just thinking about it. We got excited, jumped in the jets and took off – it was only about 90 miles to the target. We were flying at 450 knots, so we got there in about ten minutes.

'One thing I do remember is that the weather started to come in, which meant that we had an 8000-ft overcast in the KTO. As a result of the Iraqi air defence threat, we did not fly our much-rehearsed low-altitude approach to perform a ten-degree pop-up dive attack. Because of the IR SAM threat, our plan had originally been to employ high-dive tactics, but these had to be ruled out as well on 17 January due to the overcast.

'We loaded the bomb data into the computer using the brick insert system (a mission planning hard drive device that newer AV-8Bs had

MJ-1 'jammers' are used to lift Mk 83 1000-lb bombs so that squadron armourers can secure the weapons to the underwing pylons of 'Cat 12' (BuNo 163674) on the ramp at King Abdul Aziz during *Desert Storm* (*Dick White*)

which allowed the pilot to insert all mission data into the mission computer with the push of the "accept" button), which was much faster than the previous system that relied on manual insertion using the Up Front Display.

'We flew out over the water and were soon talking to the OV-10 that had spotted the target. I have to admit that we were all excited. The adrenalin was flowing, and we were glad to be the first AV-8Bs to launch. Anyone that is in that business wants to be first. Everyone was pumped – the troops, the maintenance guys and, of course, our four pilots!

'We did a shallow dive and used the CCIP "death dot" in an east-to-west attack line from the water, splitting our runs up so that we did not all come in from the same heading. I received a coordinate from the FAC in the OV-10 and entered it into my jet's INS. The Bronco crew had also marked the target with a five-inch Zuni white phosphorous rocket.

'We started our run and broke out through the clouds. It was surreal. The Iraqi artillery was still firing from right where the OV-10 told us it would be – I could see the marking rocket still smoking. I was at about 8000 ft and in a 20-degree dive. You could see everything – the guns, the people and the trench lines. I radioed "I will take the far western half", and I told squadronmate Dino Peros, who was leading the other pair, to hit the remaining guns. We were each armed with four Mk 83 1000-lb bombs, and we broke our runs up into two passes, each jet dropping two bombs per pass. I dropped and then climbed back up into the overcast and headed out over the water.

'The OV-10 crew was videotaping the strike, and they gave us commentary, just as they did during our peacetime combined arms exercises. It was a picture-perfect strike, and that was how the mission went. VMA-311 had a lot of experienced guys who had plenty of flight time, and they knew how to do their job. We had been flying together for a few years out of Yuma, so we were comfortable conducting such a precision strike. We dropped on the guns and the OV-10 confirmed this.

'I had nothing on my radar warning receiver (RWR) to indicate either tracking or lock on from AAA or SAM radars. We had either surprised them or they were not prepared for an attack. If we had been shot at we would have left, but when we did not receive fire we went back and strafed the positions with our 25 mm cannons. We made two passes for a total of four runs. We felt comfortable, as no one was shooting at us. We had confirmation of this from the OV-10.

'Upon leaving the area, we realised that we had destroyed the target. We had flown the first Harrier II attacks of the war and we were all pumped! Everyone was okay and no one was hit – and the war was on. As we came back and made the break into the landing pattern, everyone

The air war began on the night of 16/17 January 1991, and a few hours later, just after dawn on the 17th, a Marine Corps OV-10 spotted an Iraqi artillery battery shelling the Saudi town of Ras al Khafji and the nearby oil refinery. Despite poor weather, the AV-8Bs were called from alert to silence the shelling, the jets being flown by (from left to right) Maj Cary Branch (VMA-311 XO) and Capts Nelson Alberts, Frank Smith and Dino Peros. Maj Branch commented, 'We were glad to be the first to launch. We did about a twenty-degree diving attack and used CCIP "death dot" mode on an east-west attack line from the water. We started our run and broke through the cloud base, and what we saw below us was surreal. The Iraqi artillery was still firing as I dropped and went back up into the clouds. It was a near picture-perfect strike.' Together, the four pilots attacked and silenced the Iraqi artillery battery that was firing on Coalition forces, expending some 16 Mk 83 bombs and more than 1000 rounds of 25 mm cannon fire. This was the first attack mission flown by AV-8Bs in *Desert Storm* (*Dick White*) at King Abdul Aziz was lined upon the ramp. I had flown Harrier II "demos" at airshows and it looked like one of those at our base. People were everywhere. When we landed and taxied in the troops went nuts as they saw the arming wires hanging down from the underwing pylons – we had dropped our bombs!'

Further strikes followed on 17 January, and the effectiveness of these attacks was subsequently confirmed in a letter from Lt Col R M Barry, executive officer of I MEF's 2nd Surveillance, Reconnaissance, Intelligence Group, to the Commanding General of 2nd MAW;

'The purpose of this correspondence is to relate, as a matter of continuity, an incident that occurred in combat in the hope of recognising the responsible parties.

'I was posted by the commanding general, I MEF, on 25 December 1990 as the commanding officer of the forward operating base north of Ras Al Khafji. Our command post controlled eight outposts manned by US Army Special Forces, reconnaissance Marines and SEALs. Our mission was surveillance, reconnaissance of obstacles and enemy movement, and preparation for cross-border operations.

'On 17 January 1991, hostilities commenced and Iraqi artillery began firing on my command post at the desalination plant, grids TM475572. I was outside friendly artillery range, and thus began looking for air support. The enemy had a 152 mm self-propelled battery at grids TM445632 and was firing flat trajectory into my position with effect. At approximately 0930 hrs, two A-10s were diverted by the Air Force Airborne Command and Control Center to support me. The A-10s checked in and indicated that cloud cover and a briefed SA-8 threat were causing them to return to base. Essentially, they left me and my force without any air support.

'Next, four Harrier IIs checked in and were "looking for work". I identified the target and indicated that they were firing, and to look for the smoke. The Harrier IIs attacked the target with extreme bravery and aggressiveness, dropping 12 to 16 250-lb bombs, setting off all stored ammunition. They repeatedly attacked the battery, coming straight from the top dropping one bomb at a time for accuracy. Several hundred anti-aircraft artillery rounds were fired at the Harrier IIs, but they continued to press the attack, expending all ordnance and firing their internal guns. The battery was completely destroyed, and I could see pieces of artillery flying backwards into the air. Later, we took 11 prisoners – they were bleeding from the ears and noses, indicating their battery had been wiped out by aeroplanes. All their guns were destroyed and the commander had been killed.

'I personally witnessed this, and would recommend that flight schedules be researched to find the squadron and pilots who dropped on grids TM445632 at approximately 0930 hrs on 17 January 1991. Not only was it a superlative display of airmanship and bombing accuracy, but it took a lot of plain "old guts", as the fire was intense. I feel compelled to chase this one down, as they saved my group of 34 combined forces personnel from further bombardment, as we had already sustained two-and-a-half hours of the same, and enemy accuracy was improving.

'I would, at a minimum, recommend that Distinguished Flying Crosses be awarded to all four plots, as their on station time and attack lasted at least 30 minutes, and the overall effect was that the enemy rarely ever fired artillery in the daylight again until the offensive commenced.'

Following the success over Ras al Khafji, from 18 January the AV-8B units 'commenced steady day-to-day attack operations' according to Lt Col Dick White. 'This continued every day until 27 February, when the ceasefire was called. The ground offensive had commenced just four days earlier, and we flew missions around the clock in support of advancing Marines and Coalition forces. By the time *Desert Storm* was over our maintenance people had been turning aircraft for 60 days without a break. We had commenced intensive support preparations before the start of the air campaign to make sure that the Harrier IIs were capable of sustaining such a mission rate. We conducted flight operations 24 hours a day throughout the conflict, and we always had sufficient jets available to execute planned strikes'.

Lt Col Cary Branch commented on VMA-311's early operations in *Desert Storm*;

'The transition to day-to-day strike ops was pretty smooth. I cannot say it was routine, but in some ways it was easy. After our first few combat missions we had all been shot at, and we knew the ingress and egress profiles and tactics to perform in order to minimise our exposure to AAA and SAMs. Every mission was a bit different. Some were easy and no one shot at you, while others were really tough, but it all became routine after a short while. Often we would fly two back-to-back missions, refuelling and rearming at King Abdul Aziz or Tanajib, and then go straight back into action. Other pilots in the unit would use this time to catch up on their rest so that they could pick up the slack when we were off.

'We would get the CENTAF ATO and plan our mission schedule around it. CENTAF assigned the plan and kill zones for USAF, US Navy/Marine Corps and Coalition crews.

'Whenever we were flying missions over the KTO, we were ready for action. I never felt that it was like flying at home from Yuma. Initially, we thought we were going to fly large multi-section strikes – four- and eight-aeroplane coordinated strikes. Lt Col White would lead one and I would take another. We planned to fly these missions with a Sidewinder on each jet for self-defence. We were also short of AN/ALQ-164 defensive electronic countermeasures (DECM) pods, which protected the AV-8Bs from radar-directed SAMs and AAA. This in turn meant that only one aircraft per four-jet formation would carry a DECM jamming pod.

'Within a few days of the conflict starting we went from four or more jets in a formation to a two-aeroplane strike mentality. We quit carrying the Sidewinders and jamming pods and instead loaded the AV-8Bs with as much ordnance as we could carry. At this time we were mostly flying in two-aircraft sections, and we would get a feel for the target we had been assigned upon our arrival in the KTO. Aside from our underwing ordnance, we always had the GAU-12/A cannon and 300 rounds of 25 mm ammunition.

'It took the Iraqis a while to figure out that they could no longer send out daylight convoys, as we were blowing them up. We usually employed Mk 82 Low-Drag General Purpose (LDGP) 500-lb bombs and Mk 20 Rockeye II cluster bomb units, with the occasional 1000-lb Mk 83 LDGP also being dropped. I personally liked the Rockeye II, as it was a good weapon for the types of targets we were going after – tanks, rocket launchers and artillery. After a week, all of the IrAF airfields had been blown to crap and known defensive positions were being bombed regularly. This continued until just before the ground war kicked off. Then we went into battlefield prep mode.'

More than 70 percent of the AV-8B sorties flown during the war were against ground order of battle targets in southern Kuwait. A high-angle dive delivery against a target that had been visually acquired was the usual mode of attack for a Harrier II pilot. As noted earlier in this chapter, the AV-8B boasted sophisticated computing weapons delivery systems that included the nose-mounted ARBS and HUD, which provided the pilot with continuous targeting cues for bomb delivery and gun attacks.

The mostly widely employed weapon was the Mk 20 Rockeye II CBU. Following release, at a preset time of fall, the Mk 20 casing would split open and release 247 Mk 118 armour-piercing bomblets. These would cover the ground in a wide pattern, much the same as a shotgun blast. Each of the 1.32-lb bomblets would explode on impact, blasting through seven inches of armour and spreading lethal fragments in all directions. A number of bomblets landed in the relatively soft desert sand that abounded in the KTO, however, resulting in detonation failure – an estimated ten percent of those dropped suffered this fate.

The second most used weapon was the 500-lb Mk 82 LDGP bomb. Both conical-fin and high-drag Snakeye Mk 82 bombs were carried, with the latter version often having its fins banded shut. Only a small number of the larger 1000-lb Mk 83 conical-finned LDGPs were carried by Harrier IIs, as they were most often employed by A-6s and F/A-18s.

At around 1000 hrs on 28 January 1991 VMA-311 suffered the first combat casualty of *Desert Storm*. A flight of AV-8Bs from the unit had struggled to locate a rocket launcher near the coast of Kuwait, and when Capt Michael C Berryman returned to the target area once again to conduct another visual search, his jet (BuNo 163518) was hit by an infrared shoulder-launched SAM. Berryman successfully ejected and was captured, although his prisoner of war (PoW) status was not known until the conflict had ended.

'We knew we were getting shot at by AAA and SAMs, but early in the air war no one had been hit', explained Lt Col Cary Branch. 'Capt Berryman getting shot down during the second week of the air war was

VMA-311 'Tomcats' AV-8Bs head a line up of Harrier IIs at King Abdul Aziz during *Desert Storm*. The jet in the foreground is armed with Mk 20 Rockeye II canisters, and more can be seen on a munitions trailer parked between the second and third jets in the row. After the CBU had been released, at a preset time (usually 1.2 to four seconds) the casing of the canister would split open, allowing the 247 bomblets inside to disperse. These would cover the target area like a shotgun blast, each 1.32-lb Mk 118 bomblet exploding on impact. The shrapnel from the weapon could cut through seven inches of armour (*Peter Mersky collection*)

a reality wake-up call for all of us. The CO talked with all the pilots, and he told them not to take extra risks when it came to attacking targets. As the XO, it was my job to pack up all of Capt Berryman's stuff to send it home, and to talk to his wife. We thought he was dead since we had seen no 'chute.'

According to Col Bioty, by late January 'the Marine Corps was becoming very concerned about the dynamic battlefield situations the ATO could not plan for. We had aircraft on strip alert, and that was recorded on the ATO. These jets gave us a modicum of flexibility when it came to answering emergency calls for CAS. For example, I flew a mission on 29 January that was directed by a FastFAC F/A-18D. We saw a conglomeration of vehicles milling around. We were at 15,000 ft and still taking AAA. I had six Rockeye IIs and my wingman had four 1000-lb bombs. My wingman saw a lot of AAA fire and he aborted his first run, but we hit the vehicles minutes later after approaching them from a different direction.

'After we landed, I called Maj Gen Moore, who asked me how things were going? I told him that all three sorties had gone well. He replied *"Three"*? I told him that I had attacked the target directly from King Abdul Aziz, then landed at Tanajib and refuelled and rearmed, before taking off again. Having hit the vehicles once more, I then returned to Tanajib and got more fuel and bombs, attacked the target once again and then came home.

'These were the only missions I flew during the Battle of Khafji, and the whole event did not seem that big a deal during the war. Later, however, the clash took on greater significance. Taking place between 29 and 31 January, the AV-8Bs helped ground forces repel the Iraqi Army's 29th Mechanised Brigade as it attacked Khafji and three other points along the Saudi border.

'On the 29th we had started getting reports of movement, followed by requests for air support, so the alert Harrier IIs were launched. The round-the-clock mission cycle remained pretty much constant for the next 72 hours. Later, the ground forces told us we had achieved some good hits on vehicles with bombs and strafing.'

Lt Col Cary Branch also flew sorties during the Khafji operation, as well as numerous missions against various targets in the KTO in the opening days of the campaign;

Armed with Mk 20 Rockeye II canisters on the outboard pylons and Mk 82 bombs inboard, a quartet of VMA-311 aircraft taxi out from the ramp at King Abdul Aziz at the start of yet another mission over the KTO in late January 1991 (*Dick White*)

'We had names for all of the places we targeted, and after landing we would brief the intel guys and give them our HUD tapes. We would tell them we had had a couple of SAMs fired at us, or that the "golf course" was real hot with AAA today. I was lucky as I never got hit. This was just as well, as one of the downsides of the jet was its survivability. Everything is in the same spot – the hot nozzles, three hydraulic lines, fuel and engine, with the pilot sat in front of it all.

'The weapons system fitted to the Harrier II was such that if you put the pipper on the target and used the ARBS, the bombs were going to go where you told them to. I do not recall seeing a difference between using a slick Mk 82 or a banded Mk 82 Snakeye, as the weapons system did what we told it to do. With the Rockeye II, once we got the revised software, we could time the opening of the canisters so that we could use similar delivery tactics, dive angles, altitudes and airspeed for the CBU as we did for the Mk 82. We would go in as steep as we could and go out as fast as we could.

'I preferred the Rockeye IIs over the Mk 82s simply because they were more reliable. For the soft targets such as dirt berms protecting fuel trucks or rocket launchers, the Rockeye II was perfect because the hundreds of bomblets within each canister gave you a better kill ratio thanks to their larger footprint when compared with the Mk 82. That was why the Rockeye II was the AV-8B pilot's weapon of choice in the kill boxes.

'About three days before the ground war commenced, instead of working over kill zones we started targeting trench lines filled with oil. Senior Coalition commanders were worried that the enemy would fire up the oil when our mechanised troops tried to pass through them. We were now charged with neutralising this threat as part of our battlefield-shaping mission. We would approach the trench lines in a ten-degree dive and hit them with Mk 82 Snakeyes and napalm.

'I could see Iraqi troops firing at us as we flew these battlefield prep missions. We were really low, and they were firing at us with assault rifles and numerous other weapons. Speed was out greatest defence in these situations, and we would approach the target at 550 knots – as fast as

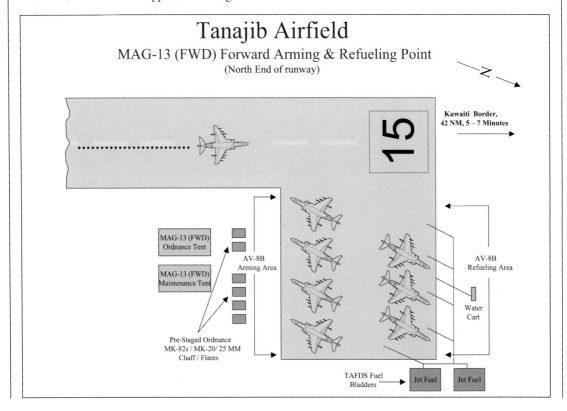

the jet would go – at a height of just 20 ft, and we would never re-attack. These were "First pass, Haul-ass" sorties. We flew these missions for two or three days solid. We were dropping old lot number Snakeyes and napalm, and we were frustrated as we had a lot of duds.'

Lt Col Branch also explained that VMA-311 flew a small number of nocturnal missions in the lead up to the ground war, which commenced at 0400 hrs on 24 February;

'The objective of our night missions before the ground war was to hit targets along the border, and we relied on laser marking from ground forces and, in a few cases, A-6 Intruders. We couldn't see anything on the desert floor from our day attack Harrier IIs, so we had to use flares or laser designation. I flew 44 missions in *Desert Storm*, and fewer than ten were night missions. We were not all that accurate at night. The A-6s were great, and some of the F/A-18s had forward-looking infrared sensors (FLIRs), but we were very limited in the day attack AV-8Bs.

'One thing that really helped us in the kill boxes was when the FastFAC F/A-18D two-seaters (of VMFA(AW)-121) showed up. We were out there working a kill zone using our ARBS TV from medium altitudes, and although the system had magnification, we were not sure if the things we were seeing on the screen were real targets or ones that had already been blown up. So we droned around talking amongst ourselves before going ahead and bombing the targets in any case! When the F/A-18Ds showed up in late January things quickly improved. The Weapons System Officers in the back of the two-seat Hornets had both binoculars and a FLIR with which to identify targets. They would mark them with rockets or talk us onto them via communications procedures that we had quickly standardised with the Hornet squadron. From then on we arrived over a kill box with a set of known targets that were valid, and the FastFAC crew could confirm that we had hit them accurately. There was a monumental increase in the number of kills we were now achieving.

'Once the ground war commenced in earnest, I believe I only flew three missions that fitted the textbook definition of CAS. This was where you checked in with a ground FAC and he said "Okay", he marked the target with artillery and I popped up and released my ordnance in close proximity of friendly troops. So we went from the kill boxes to battlefield prep (just before the ground war started) to traditional CAS on the last days of the conflict.

'The Iraqis were fleeing Kuwait as fast as they could, heading north. It was a chaotic free-for-all. There was a cloud layer at about 8000 ft from the oil well fires lit by Saddam's troops as they fled, whilst above it the sky was sunny and clear. I recall popping above the cloud layer and enjoying the sunshine. Once below 8000 ft,

Lt Col Dick White poses in front of his AV-8B, which has been loaded with Mk 77 napalm canisters. During the Iran-Iraq War, the Iraqis found that trenches filled with an oil-gas mixture served as a good deterrent to massed-wave attacks by Iranian infantry when ignited. Iraqi troops duly dug trenches along the Saudi-Kuwaiti border and around their defensive fortifications and filled them with flammable materials. AV-8B pilots dropped around 400 Mk 77 napalm weapons into the trenches just before and during the ground war to eliminate these threats. Mk 77 attack missions were not popular as they required a low-level delivery, which made pilots vulnerable to ground fire. Napalm was also an inaccurate weapon, and each canister had a drag index of 5.7 – four times greater than a Mk 82 bomb (*Dick White*)

however, the KTO reminded me of the opening scenes from the film *Terminator*, where you saw machines, smoke and fires everywhere. It resembled Hell on the ground.

'We were briefed to run in on targets from the east and pull away to the west so as not to hit other attack aircraft in the area like A-10s and F/A-18s. Midair collisions posed a serious threat to all Coalition aircraft in-theatre as there was limited command and control for the many jets overflying the battle zone. Aircraft were operating all over the KTO, and although I never heard of a close midair involving jets from King Abdul Aziz, you routinely saw other aircraft whilst flying in Kuwaiti airspace and heard incessant chatter on the radios. I recall seeing A-10 guys up on my left bombing fleeing Iraqi vehicles and a Hornet popping out nearby through the overcast. It was surreal.

'When I observed Iraqi forces fleeing Kuwait I thought to myself that I probably wouldn't die in *Desert Storm*. Admittedly, we had lost five Harrier IIs, but then we had flown a lot of missions at medium to low altitudes over the KTO. As each day passed it seemed that there were fewer and fewer SAMs and AAA fired at us. I do not want to say we were cocky, but we got very good at what we were doing. Some guys got hit at the end of the campaign supporting the ground war, but the primary reason for us being there was to support the mechanised troops. The air war prior to the liberation of the KTO was intense. However, Marine aviators adopted a completely different mindset once we knew that our brethren on the ground were getting shot at. We employed dangerous low-altitude tactics during the four-day ground war in order to protect the Coalition advance into Kuwait.'

Col Bioty also flew a handful of CAS sorties in VMA-331 jets during the final days of *Desert Storm*;

'I can tell you that of the 33 missions I completed, only three fit the classic definition of CAS. That is, within the fire-support coordination line and in terminal control with a FAC in support of friendly troops.

VMA-311 AV-8B BuNo 163517 is flown low over the KTO at the end of *Desert Storm*. As Iraqi troops pulled out of Kuwait they set more than 600 oil wells on fire. The burning oil reduced battlefield visibility and created an environmental disaster (*John Bioty*)

I would say about 15 percent of all AV-8B sorties involved traditional CAS. Many people said later that we had not needed much CAS in *Desert Storm*, so the Marine Corps AV-8B concept had failed. My response to that is the fact that we did not have to do much CAS was a good thing, not a bad thing. Having an aeroplane like the AV-8B that could perform multiple missions, and do them well, was a good thing. You try and attrite the enemy as far forward as possible with BAI sorties. This worked very well. Most to the enemy was demoralised and affected by continuous bombing and battlefield shaping for 38 days prior to the ground war. However, when you had to do CAS, you had to do it well.'

Another pilot who flew with VMA-311 was then Capt (later Lt Col) Michael Hile, who joined the unit just prior to it deploying to Saudi Arabia;

'I was flying with VMA-214 at MCAS Yuma, and had just started to train for the AV-8B night attack jet, when Saddam Hussein invaded Kuwait. VMA-311 was working up on base for a deployment to Iwakuni at the time, and it seemed almost overnight that the unit was redirected to prepare for redeployment to the Middle East. It left Yuma within a week of being given notice that it was deploying, and some of the junior pilots in the squadron were transferred out and more experienced pilots recruited in their place. Amongst the latter was Maj Bill "Mellow" Williams, who was brought in as the operations officer. He asked me if I was interested in joining VMA-311 for the Middle East deployment.

'I had been studying night attack tactics and systems for months with VMA-214, and once I joined the "Tomcats" I had to re-learn day attack avionics. I recall that flying the day attack aircraft at night was very restrictive, but both jets handled the same way in the V/STOL environment, as both units still focused their training on preparing pilots for forward deployment utilising small airfields close to the battle zone in order to reduce response times for troops in contact with the enemy.

'Once in Saudi Arabia, all of our tactical training was geared towards us flying low-threat, high-altitude missions, either in two- or four-ship formations, flown in a combat spread with visual lookout. Our training and combat operations focused on CAS or self-controlled kill box tactics, the latter being a form of battlefield air interdiction. Within a few days of combat commencing, Harrier IIs were also utilised in what became known as "push CAS", where jets would get airborne and fly a CAS mission as directed by a FAC. If they were told en route that their services were no longer required, pilots would divert to a kill box mission.

'Without GPS, and flying over the KTO's huge expanses of

Col John 'Hunter' Bioty (CO of MAG-13 (Forward)) and his wingman, Capt Mark 'Rude' Everman (of VMA-231), take a break between sorties at the Tanajib forward operating site while their jets are rearmed and refuelled. Col Bioty, who flew 33 strike missions during the conflict, was fulsome in his praise of the support units within his command. 'I cannot say enough about the Seabees and Marine Wing Support Squadrons who worked with us – they were worth their weight in gold. They build up a forward operating strip at Tanajib for rearming and refuelling using a narrow runway and aluminium matting for turnaround areas' (*John Bioty*)

The view from the AV-8B 'office' in the form of a self-portrait taken by Lt Col Dick White, who explained, 'We generally had 20 to 30 minutes of loiter time over the target areas, depending upon the ordnance load. If you were carrying six Rockeye II or napalm canisters it was like flying with a barn door open out there. If you got the ordnance off in a hurry, fuel was not much of a problem. The Mk 82 and Mk 83 slick general purpose bombs had a much lower drag penalty than the Rockeye II. For what we were doing, though, the Mk 20 was the preferred weapon.' The most common attack loading for the AV-8B in the conflict was six Mk 82 freefall 500-lb bombs or six Mk 20 Rockeye II CBUs on single racks on wing stations' 1, 2, 3, 5, 6 and 7. The drag index of a single Mk 82 on a parent rack was only 1.4, while the Mk 20 was 4.2, so the AV-8B had greater acceleration, range and loiter time when carrying freefall 500 'pounders' than it did when loaded with Rockeye IIs (*Dick White*)

featureless terrain, pinpoint navigation proved to be extremely challenging. F/A-18D FastFACs came to our aid, guiding us to known enemy locations.

'The principal weapon used by the Harrier II was the Mk 20 Rockeye II CBU, although we also occasionally expended napalm and Mk 82/83 bombs. After they were dropped, the Mk 20 canisters would break open either 1.2 or four seconds later, according to their fusing. The latter could not be extended due to avionic limitations in the Harrier IIs. This in turn meant that we were forced to drop the CBUs from lower altitudes than other jets armed with Rockeye IIs, and I believe that this was the primary reason why the AV-8B suffered a higher loss rate than any other American strike aircraft committed to *Desert Storm*.

'Early on AAA was seen on almost every sortie, although after a few days of pounding from the air flak was seen only in pockets. Electronic indications for SA-2/3/6 SAMs were occasionally received, but I believe I saw only one SA-2 launch off in the distance. The real threat was from passive IR SAMs – SA-7/14/16 – and I believe all the AV-8B losses were due to these missiles.'

According to Capt Hile's CO, Lt Col Dick White, 'I do not recall a Harrier II being fired on by a radar-guided missile. There were, however, OV-10, A-6 and F/A-18 crews that said they were fired at by radar-guided SAMs or SA-2s launched without radar control. We did take losses to IR SAMs – SA-7/14/16 and the larger SA-9. According to pilots who survived being shot down by a man-portable missile, they never saw the weapon that was fired at them. I had a similar experience, for on at least two occasions my wingman called me and said a missile had just flown by my aircraft, having failed to guide.

'In an effort to defeat the IR missiles we used plenty of chaff and flare expendables as standard operating procedure. When we came off bombing a target, the chaff and flares were liberally pumped out. That was our most vulnerable time as we tried to get back up to a safe altitude, out of the SAM and AAA zone. And this is when it seems that all of the AV-8B losses were suffered, coming off the target.

'The Harrier IIs did not use in-flight refuelling during *Desert Storm*. The other arrack aircraft had to use tankers, for they were based further south than us. We generally had 20 to 30 minutes of loiter time over the target area, depending on our ordnance load. If we were carrying six Rockeye IIs or napalm canisters, it was essentially like flying with a barn door open. If you got the ordnance off in a hurry, fuel was not much of a problem. Mk 82 and 83 slick LDGPs produced far less drag than the Rockeye IIs, but for what we were doing in-theatre, the Mk 20 was the preferred weapon.

A 'Tomcats' AV-8B flies over the famous Kuwait City spires after *Desert Storm* had ended. VMA-311 was the first Marine Corps unit into the Middle East and among the last squadrons to depart. It did not return home to MCAS Yuma until 18 April 1991 (*John Bioty*)

'We finally returned home on 18 April. We flew 19 aircraft into the break at Yuma, and the next day 18 of them were parked on the flightline fully mission capable. That is quite a testimonial to the Harrier II, the team who built the aircraft and our team that supported it. We were all impressed with the jet's reliability, its accuracy as a bomber and its ability to do the job it was designed for. Ground commanders and the media were impressed too. Whilst in-theatre we were routinely asked whether we could move forward into the KTO if required, and I would reply "Absolutely! Give me a stretch of road or a parking lot, even one made of aluminium matting, and we will operate and support you." The USAF and units tied to the big airfields could not say that. I think the Harrier II acquitted itself very well in *Desert Storm*. We opened a lot of eyes over there by showing people exactly what the jet could do in combat.'

VMA-311 won the Marine Corps Aviation Association's Lawson H M Sanderson Award for the Marine Attack Squadron of the Year in 1991, the citation accompanying this accolade stating, 'VMA-311 was selected for achieving a superior level of performance for a Marine attack squadron. Its record of safety, operational readiness and combat success in the austere, demanding environment of Southwest Asia is a truly remarkable and noteworthy accomplishment. As the most forward fixed-wing squadron in support of *Desert Storm*, the "Tomcats" flew 1017 sorties totalling 1200 combat hours.'

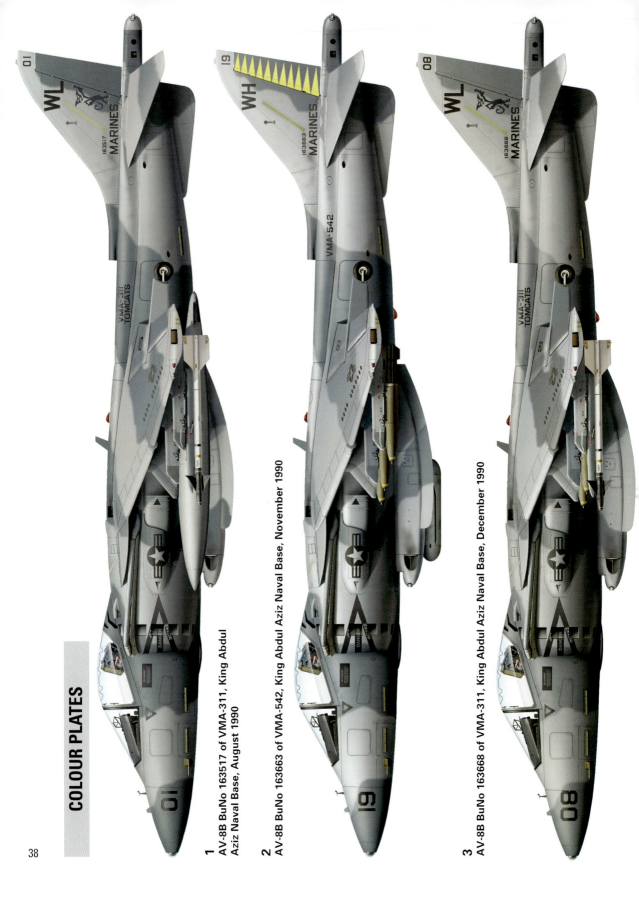

COLOUR PLATES

1
AV-8B BuNo 163517 of VMA-311, King Abdul
Aziz Naval Base, August 1990

2
AV-8B BuNo 163663 of VMA-542, King Abdul Aziz Naval Base, November 1990

3
AV-8B BuNo 163668 of VMA-311, King Abdul Aziz Naval Base, December 1990

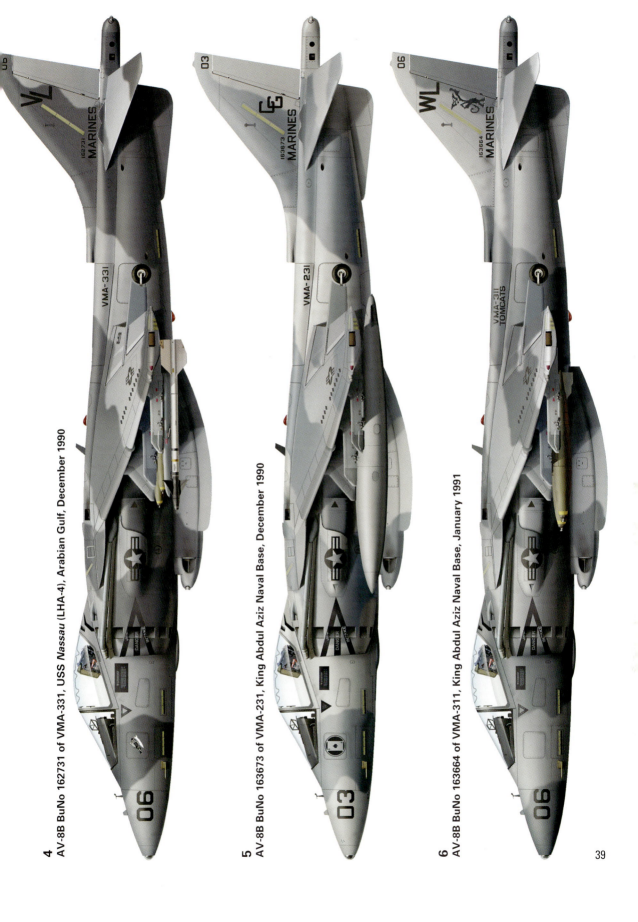

4
AV-8B BuNo 162731 of VMA-331, USS *Nassau* (LHA-4), Arabian Gulf, December 1990

5
AV-8B BuNo 163673 of VMA-231, King Abdul Aziz Naval Base, December 1990

6
AV-8B BuNo 163664 of VMA-311, King Abdul Aziz Naval Base, January 1991

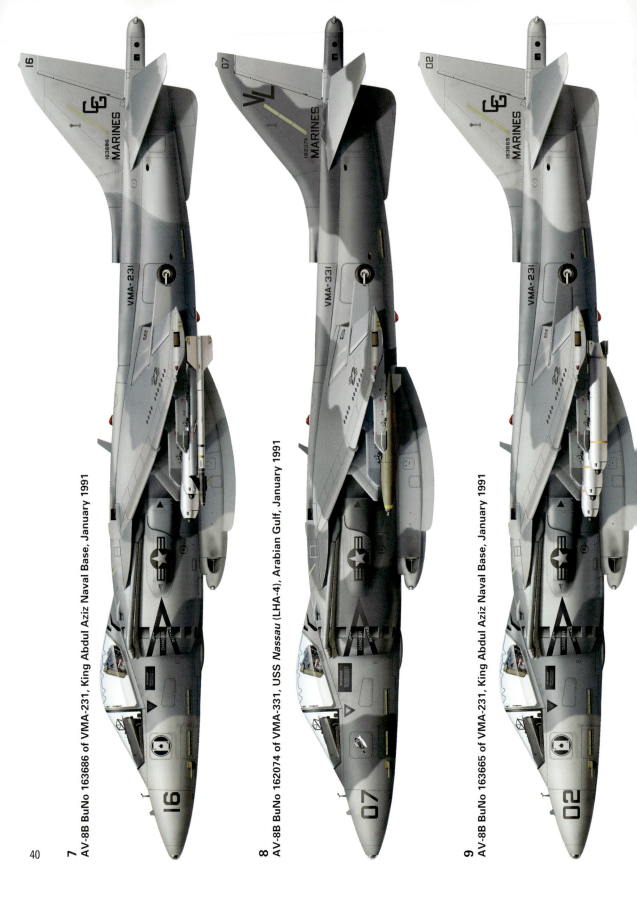

7
AV-8B BuNo 163686 of VMA-231, King Abdul Aziz Naval Base, January 1991

8
AV-8B BuNo 162074 of VMA-331, USS *Nassau* (LHA-4), Arabian Gulf, January 1991

9
AV-8B BuNo 163665 of VMA-231, King Abdul Aziz Naval Base, January 1991

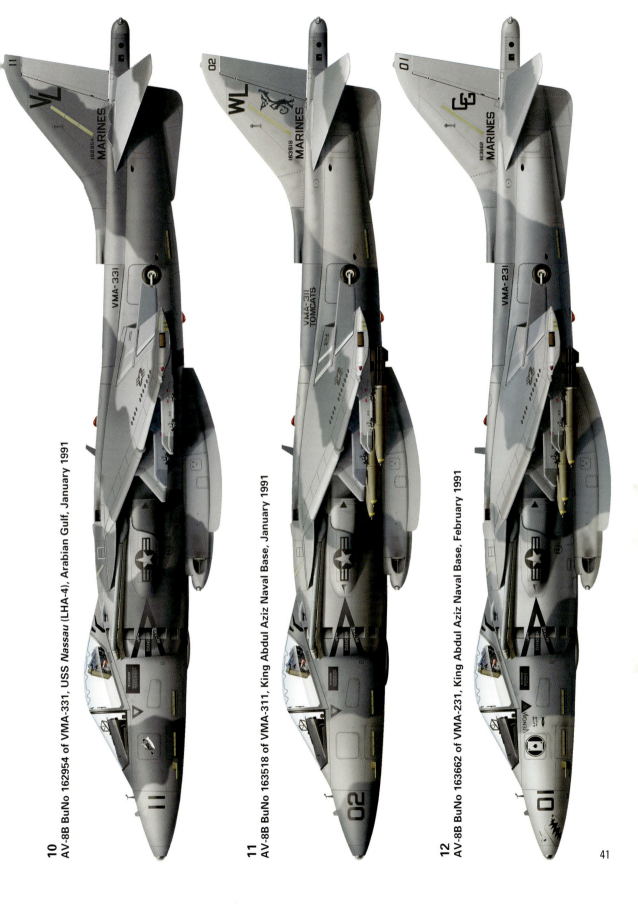

10
AV-8B BuNo 162954 of VMA-331, USS *Nassau* (LHA-4), Arabian Gulf, January 1991

11
AV-8B BuNo 163518 of VMA-311, King Abdul Aziz Naval Base, January 1991

12
AV-8B BuNo 163662 of VMA-231, King Abdul Aziz Naval Base, February 1991

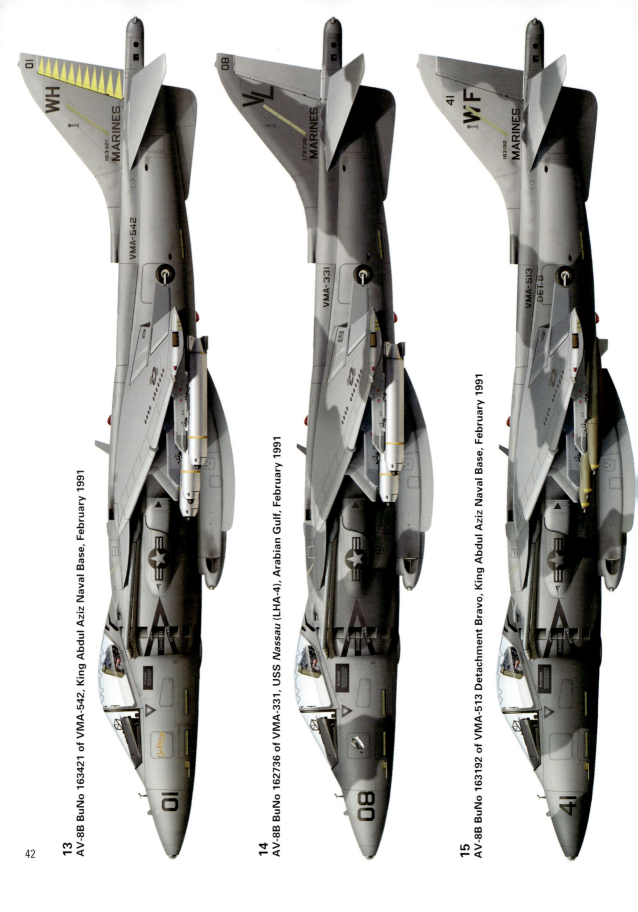

42

13
AV-8B BuNo 163421 of VMA-542, King Abdul Aziz Naval Base, February 1991

14
AV-8B BuNo 162736 of VMA-331, USS *Nassau* (LHA-4), Arabian Gulf, February 1991

15
AV-8B BuNo 163192 of VMA-513 Detachment Bravo, King Abdul Aziz Naval Base, February 1991

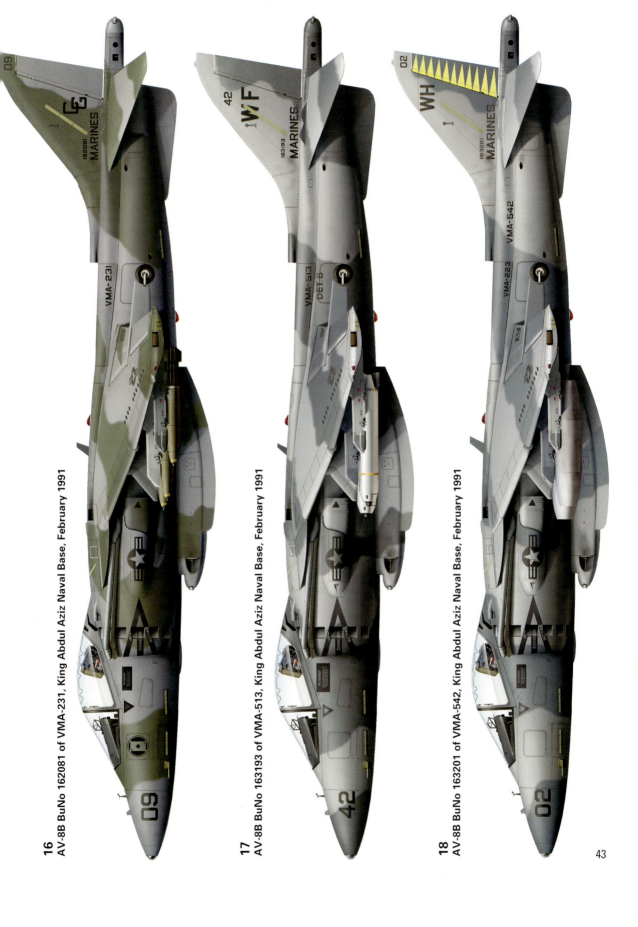

16
AV-8B BuNo 162081 of VMA-231, King Abdul Aziz Naval Base, February 1991

17
AV-8B BuNo 163193 of VMA-513, King Abdul Aziz Naval Base, February 1991

18
AV-8B BuNo 163201 of VMA-542, King Abdul Aziz Naval Base, February 1991

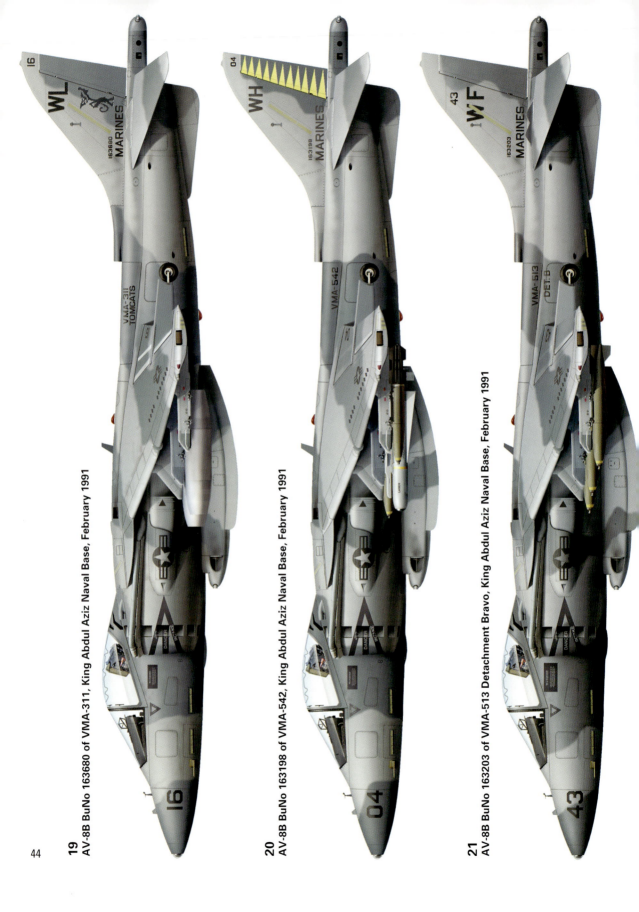

44

19
AV-8B BuNo 163680 of VMA-311, King Abdul Aziz Naval Base, February 1991

20
AV-8B BuNo 163198 of VMA-542, King Abdul Aziz Naval Base, February 1991

21
AV-8B BuNo 163203 of VMA-513 Detachment Bravo, King Abdul Aziz Naval Base, February 1991

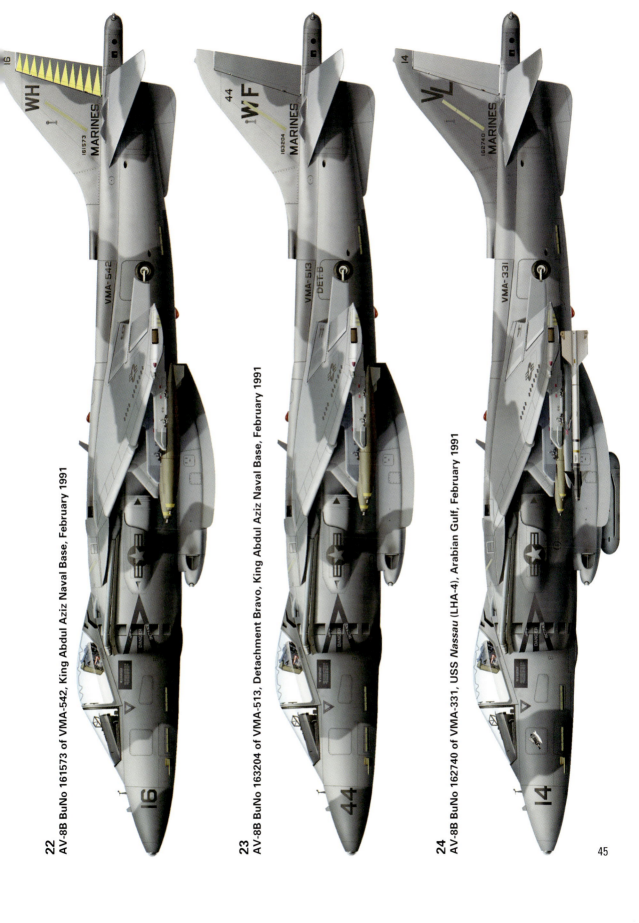

22
AV-8B BuNo 161573 of VMA-542, King Abdul Aziz Naval Base, February 1991

23
AV-8B BuNo 163204 of VMA-513, Detachment Bravo, King Abdul Aziz Naval Base, February 1991

24
AV-8B BuNo 162740 of VMA-331, USS *Nassau* (LHA-4), Arabian Gulf, February 1991

VMA-542

VMA-542 'Tigers' was formed as VMF(N)-542 in March 1944, the unit being assigned the nightfighter mission with F6F-5N Hellcats. Redesignated VMF(AW)-542 in 1948, the squadron saw more action with the F7F-3N Tigercat in the Korean War and flew thousands of sorties over Vietnam and Laos with the F-4B Phantom II between 1965 and 1970. In 1972 VMFA-542 became VMA-542 when it transitioned to the AV-8A Harrier. The unit flew the aircraft with distinction for the next 14 years, consecutively winning the V/STOL Squadron of the Year award in the late 1970s. In May 1986, VMA-542 transitioned to the AV-8B day attack aircraft.

Since the end of the Korean War, the Marine Corps have regularly deployed units to Japan and Okinawa to strengthen western Pacific (WESTPAC) defences. In late 1989 VMA-542 was posted to Iwakuni for a six-month tour under the Unit Deployment Program (UDP) and returned to Cherry Point in May 1990. As is common for squadrons involved in the UDP, the 'Tigers' left their 20 AV-8Bs in Iwakuni with the relieving squadron, VMA-231, and took over the jets flown by the 'Aces' upon their return to Cherry Point.

Lt Col Theodore 'Ted' Herman first flew VMA-542 in its AV-8A days, and he assumed command of the squadron in September 1989;

'We were adjusting to being home at Cherry Point and making all of the post-deployment changes of personnel and training when, on 7 August, MAG-32 CO Col John Dempsey told me that the unit had to be ready within two weeks for service in the Middle East in support of 3rd MAW. We were ready for our "fly-away" to join MAG-70 in support of the 7th MEB in less than ten days. VMA-542 achieved this thanks to the considerable help we received from VMAT-203 and VMA-223.

'We exchanged the older birds we had inherited from VMA-231 for 20 newer aircraft that were equipped with digital fuel controls. Transferring an aeroplane is not a simple thing. It requires opening every panel on the jet and reviewing all the records because you are taking a machine from another squadron and inducting it into your own maintenance system. Fortunately, we found the AV-8Bs that we were receiving to be in good shape, bar a few exceptions pertaining to some high-time components that we had to change. This is standard procedure before embarking on a long-term deployment.

'The maintenance crews toiled around the clock so as to meet the requirements for the transatlantic flight. Jets were painted in "grey-on-grey" camouflage, support gear was accounted for, special tools procured and myriad other preparations accomplished. Support from our manufacturers, NADEP and our fellow Marines was overwhelming.

'The "Tigers" recalled pilots who had been reassigned to VMAT-203 as instructors following our return from WESTPAC, and secured several experienced pilots from other units, along with 37 enlisted support personnel, to fill out our ranks. During all of the preparations, the

"Tigers" scurried around checking out gear, NBC (nuclear, biological, chemical) equipment, rifles and pistols, tying up loose ends in their personal lives and, in the case of one of our pilots, Capt Mike "Disco" Beguelin, getting married.

'When we left Cherry Point, each of our AV-8Bs was equipped with two AIM-9M Sidewinders, 300 rounds of 25 mm ammunition, two drop tanks and two empty triple ejector racks. Pilots and maintainers were, by then, tired but ready. We had been briefed, lectured and re-briefed on every threat system known to be deployed by Iraq. Each pilot had flown the Harrier II simulators several times over desert terrain, evading missiles, interpreting returns on their RWR gear and expending weapons.

'The squadron's support equipment was packed up ready for shipment in C-141s and C-5s, which arrived on 18 August 1990. We loaded the aircraft up and were ready to depart later that same day. The main body of the squadron travelled on USAF transports. Since our troops had already left, our plane captains for the launch on 19 August were supplied by other Cherry Point units. Sgt Paris, whom I had known from previous deployments, helped me strap in, and fixed a loose connection in my radios. He gave me a red poker chip for luck before I closed the canopy. I carried that chip in my flightsuit pocket throughout the war.

'It was a dark, stormy night as we met up with our KC-10s at 2200 hrs over Pamlico Sound, north of Cherry Point. Bound for Rota, we would fly for nine hours, five of those at night, and refuel from the tankers 13 times so as to maintain a reserve to reach an alternative airfield in case of a problem. We landed at Rota at 1200 hrs local time on 20 August.

'We departed at 0700 hrs the following day and rendezvoused with the tankers over the Mediterranean Sea. Two of our aircraft had problems so they remained at Rota, where the Spanish Navy helped repair them. We flew past Italy and Greece, down the Nile, across the Red Sea and, finally, into the great pink emptiness of Saudi Arabia. We gasped silently as we crossed this monstrous desert for more than two hours before reaching Sheik Isa, the supposedly secret air base built in southern Bahrain. Landing after eight hours in the air, we were met by Maj Gen Royal Moore, CO of 3rd MAW, and were each given a cold canteen of water. It tasted mighty good as we tried to adjust to the 120°F heat! We were also met by our maintenance team, which had arrived a few

VMA-542, based at MCAS Cherry Point, North Carolina, was the second AV-8B squadron mobilised for deployment to support Operation *Desert Shield*. Here, a pair of 'Tigers'' jets refuel from a USAF KC-10 tanker on their way to Bahrain from NAS Rota on 20 August 1990. Squadron CO, Lt Col Ted Herman, recalled 'We launched from Rota and rendezvoused with the tankers over the Mediterranean Sea. We flew past Italy and Greece, down the Nile, across the Red Sea and, finally, into the great pink emptiness of Saudi Arabia. We were airborne for more than two hours before we crossed the great emptiness of the desert and reached Bahrain' (*Ted Herman*)

hours earlier. Much credit goes to the USAF's Military Airlift Command, who made sure that all of the ground-based aviation assets arrived in the region in a timely fashion.

'We had temporary quarters on the floor of a hangar and in some jam-packed BOQs (Base Officers' Quarters) on the air base. Since there was little room for all the people and jets that were being flown in to Sheik Isa, aircraft were packed in wingtip-to-wingtip and people slept in halls, on the floor of hangars and even in closets.

'Our superb maintenance team had our AV-8Bs ready for action in short order, and the morning after we arrived VMA-542 had four Harrier IIs sitting alert, armed with bombs, just in case something happened along the Saudi-Kuwait border. Our two lost jets came in several days later with a flight of A-6s.'

Over the next few weeks, US and Coalition aircraft filled every available military air base in the region to overflowing – some were even based at civil airports. At Sheik Isa, the resident Royal Bahraini Air Force F-5E/Fs and F-16C/Ds were joined by more than 100 additional jets – USAF F-4Gs and Marine Corps AV-8Bs, F/A-18s, A-6Es and EA-6Bs – which occupied all available ramp space. In addition, C-5s, C-141s and commercial jets under charter were landing every 30 minutes, bringing in more troops and supplies.

The USAF units had arrived at Sheikh Isa first, and they had duly occupied the extra hangars and most of the air-conditioned housing. Thus, the troops from VMA-542 and the other Marine Corps units assigned to MAG-70 slept in tents alongside the flightline in the heat, sand and noise. Some lucky pilots were able to find places to sleep in air-conditioned spaces, but most had to make do.

As noted in the previous chapter, within a week of arriving in Bahrain, VMA-311 moved to King Abdul Aziz Naval Base. This remained a one-squadron facility until Marine Air Base engineers and Navy Seabees could add more ramp space and additional facilities. VMA-542 therefore remained in Bahrain, with a portion of its AV-8Bs armed and pilots on alert 24 hours a day.

As Marine Corps aviation units flowed into the Middle East, on 3 September MAG-70 was split into three aircraft groups. VMA-542 came

An OV-10D forward observation aircraft from VMO-2 shares ramp space with AV-8Bs from VMA-542 at King Abdul Aziz. The Broncos of surveillance squadrons VMO-1 and -2 were equipped with a Forward Looking Infrared sensor and laser illuminator to detect and identify targets for the AV-8B and other strike aircraft. In the foreground are pods containing five-inch Zuni rockets, which were used by OV-10 crews to mark targets for bombing. The 280 mph Bronco proved vulnerable to shoulder-fired SAMs, and after an OV-10A from VMO-2 was lost on 18 January, crews were ordered to operate from orbit areas over the Arabian Gulf. Nevertheless, a second OV-10A (this time from VMO-1) was downed by a SAM on 25 February (*Peter Mersky collection*)

VMA-542's AV-8B 'Lusty 01' (BuNo 163421) is painted within a portable hangar at King Abdul Aziz. The squadron commander's aircraft, it received a unique all-grey camouflage scheme and white air intakes, as well as the nickname *Babieca* (the name of the horse ridden by 11th-century Spanish hero El Cid) (*Ted Herman*)

under the command of MAG-11, led by Col Manfred Rietsch. The group included a mix of four F/A-18 squadrons, two A-6E squadrons, an EA-6B squadron and one AV-8B squadron, all located in Bahrain. MAG-16 was formed to control the vast fleet of helicopters in-theatre, while MAG-13 (Forward), formed in October, consisted of VMA-311, with AV-8Bs, VMO-1 and -2 with OV-10s and Marine Aviation Logistics Squadron (MALS) 14 at King Abdul Aziz, under the command of Col John Bioty Jr.

In early September the pilots of VMA-542 began flying training sorties so as to become familiar with the region and to hone their tactics. Capt (later Col) Art 'Turbo' Tomassetti recalled;

'We got to Bahrain and stayed for more than two months. When we first arrived we stood alerts, as no one knew what was going to happen in Kuwait, and whether the Iraqis were going to drive further south into Saudi Arabia. Initially, we stood armed alerts, ready to launch within 15 minutes. Often, that meant we sat in the cockpit in the heat of the day. As the weeks ran on, we changed to a one-hour alert, with the pilots out of the aircraft.

'For the first few weeks of *Desert Shield* we flew only to keep pilots and crews current, and to exercise the aeroplanes so as to keep them ready for war. As we got into September, and with continued uncertainty, we started to generate training sorties once again. We found tactical bombing ranges to fly to, where we could practise missions using realistic tactics, while continuing to maintain an alert status.'

About three weeks after arriving in Bahrain, ships carrying additional support systems, spare parts and equipment docked at nearby Al Jubail Naval Base. Included in the cargo was a contingency support package for the AV-8B, as well as other critical maintenance equipment. Combined, these allowed the squadron's maintenance personnel to provide the full range of support required to keep the AV-8B operational on a long-term basis.

At this time VMA-542 consisted of 32 Marine officers and 203 enlisted personnel, two US Navy officers, four enlisted medical corpsmen and one RAF pilot on exchange. Ten pilots and 37 enlisted men had been added to the unit on the eve of departure.

Half of VMA-542's 20-strong fleet of AV-8Bs is seen here lined up at King Abdul Aziz pre-war, with the soccer stadium dominating the skyline behind them. The variety of camouflage schemes applied to 'Tigers'' aircraft can be clearly seen, this being the end result of a hasty repainting of the jets by hand prior to deployment. The two aircraft in traditional dark grey and dark green camouflage were borrowed from VMAT-203 on the eve of VMA-542's departure from MCAS Cherry Point (*Ted Herman*)

During October, while still stationed at Sheik Isa, the 'Tigers' flew 271 training sorties with its 20 jets. The following month VMA-542 moved up to King Abdul Aziz, as noted by Lt Col 'Ted' Herman;

'After nearly three months in Bahrain, we headed north to King Abdul Aziz to join VMA-311. Our new base had a single asphalt runway some 7900 ft in length. The Seabees had been busy building a parallel taxiway using AM-2 matting next to the original runway, a 150 sq ft pad for vertical landings and concrete slabs for maintenance tents and bunkers. The abandoned soccer stadium became our admin working spaces and shower facility. We lived in the parking lot, six to eight men per tent.

'Once at King Abdul Aziz we began to focus our flying on CAS training. Our close proximity to ground forces allowed us to have face-to-face meetings with them to discuss support requirements and develop tactics. We became very familiar with the terrain between us and the border of Kuwait – this would prove useful later on.'

VMA-542 was officially assigned to MAG-13 (Forward) on 5 November 1990, and it flew 267 training sorties during November while maintaining a 75 percent mission capable rate.

'At the time I thought the AV-8B day attack jet was the greatest thing flying', Col Tomassetti remarked. 'It had a good HUD, a multi-purpose display screen in the cockpit and HOTAS (hands on throttle and stick) for quick and efficient weapons and sensor selection. From a pilot's perspective, the Harrier II cockpit was ideally set up for the attack mission. The ARBS with the TV camera was good, although it had some limitations. It was not the ideal systems for all battlefield conditions, but when you could lock on to a high-contrast target, it was very accurate. I saw studies at the time that said it was even more accurate than the Hornet with radar ranging.

'We felt very comfortable with the AV-8B, knew how to use the systems and had a lot of opportunity to practise with the jet. We were experienced, well trained and had had sufficient flying time and opportunities to perform a variety of missions in the aircraft. The Harrier II was a great aeroplane for performing ground attack and CAS missions, although it took a lot of practice to fully understand V/STOL and be competent at operating it safely in this flight regime.

'Because the Harrier II required so little runway for a short take-off, we split the runway at King Abdul Aziz into two sections. The first half was for recoveries and the second half for departures. You would pull out of your parking space onto the runway and take-off from there. We did little taxiing. That allowed us to operate 60 AV-8Bs and 20 OV-10s from a single runway. We would never have been able to sustain such a high sortie rate with a conventional aeroplane in *Desert Storm*. The V/STOL capability of the jet was, therefore, used throughout the conflict.'

By year-end, VMA-542 personnel were more than ready to see a resolution to the situation in Kuwait, as Lt Col Herman explained;

'The holidays came and went and the waiting for something to happen was getting old by now. It began to appear that Saddam Hussein thought that we were bluffing, and he clearly had no intention of reacting to President Bush's 15 January 1991 deadline to pull his troops out of Kuwait. On 17 January at 0300 hrs the air war finally began, and four hours later Iraqi artillery started shelling the Saudi border town of Khafji. The Harrier IIs at King Abdul Aziz, just 80 miles south of the Kuwaiti border, were the closest units, and we were called to engage the Iraqi batteries. Our mission was simply to destroy as much Iraqi military capability as possible prior to the ground war. In the next 40 days we became combat veterans while accomplishing that mission.

'As the days progressed, our sortie rate went up from 15-20 flights per day to a sustained 30+ sorties per day – these rates apply to VMA-542 only. Landings were sequenced between take-offs. Hot refuelling pits (refuelling while the engine was running) were on the east side of the runway near its threshold. The de-arming pad was further down from that on the west side. The flow was logical, smooth and safe, allowing a section of two aircraft to launch every five minutes.

'Maintenance was done inside igloo-shaped hangars erected on concrete slabs. This gave groundcrewmen a place to work that was free from the heavy, dusty-laden "shamal" winds. The hangars also provided protected storage for our maintenance gear. Traditional Marine-green tents under camouflage netting served as home for our maintenance offices and machine shops. Engine changes, which required a crane to remove the wing and lift out the engine, were performed on the ramp in front of the hangars.

'MALS-14 set up its vans on the south side of the soccer stadium. The unit had a veritable city of machine shops, avionics test vans and supply areas to keep us maintained day and night at the intermediate level. Our tech reps, John Cox from Smiths Industries and Matt Madson and Russ Hammond from Rolls-Royce, worked from this area and from the maintenance tents on the flightline.'

In January 1991, VMA-542 flew 391 sorties and maintained a mission capable rate of 81.4 percent.

'Tigers'' groundcrew remove the canopy prior to performing maintenance on an AV-8B at King Abdul Aziz on a rare day with little wind. 'Maintenance was usually done inside igloo-shaped hangars erected on concrete slabs', Lt Col Ted Herman explained. 'This gave us a place that was out of the heavy, dusty-laden "shamal" winds and provided us with storage for our maintenance gear. Maintenance offices and shops were inside traditional Marine green tents under camouflage netting. Engine changes, which required a crane to remove the wing before the engine could be lifted out of the central fuselage, were performed on the ramp in front of the hangar. The maintenance and logistic squadron set up its vans on the south side of the soccer stadium. The unit had a veritable city of machine shops, avionics test vans and supply areas to keep us maintained night and day at the intermediate level' (*Ted Herman*)

This total included 251 combat sorties from 17 January, with an average of 17 sorties being flown per day. VMA-542 pilots dropped 330 Mk 82 bombs and 165 Mk 20 Rockeye II CBUs on Iraqi positions during this period.

'In order to increase operational flexibility and provide for surge sorties, a forward operating site was constructed at Tanajib, some 30 miles south of the Kuwait border, co-located with the helicopters of MAG-16', explained Lt Col Herman. 'AV-8Bs were rearmed and refuelled there while pilots got some brief rest, before flying another sortie. It proved to be a busy place, as each squadron surged up to 50 sorties per day. We saw no degradation of the aeroplanes as a result of the severe environment and expeditionary conditions they were subjected to.

Lt Col Ted Herman, CO of VMA-542, and Capt Ed Green prepare for an attack mission during *Desert Storm* **(***Ted Herman***)**

'During the day, pilots flew missions according to the ATO, which set a good pace. Nights became a mix of alert pilots flying a smaller number of nocturnal strikes and everyone else trying to sleep through Scud alerts. The air raid siren, signalling a Scud launch, brought sleepers to attention, forcing them to scramble for NBC gear and head to the bunkers. After a couple of weeks of harassment, we started to relax when we saw the local Patriot batteries scoring hits on the Scuds. Even so, I always worried that one of them might get through.'

Col Tomassetti recalled that the unit was initially informed the Harrier II would not get involved in the fighting until the land offensive commenced;

'Our usual job is direct support for Marine ground forces. Originally, we were told that the Harrier IIs were going to be held in reserve to support the ground war. However, when the Iraqis started firing artillery at Coalition positions on the morning of 17 January we were launched. We flew missions from that day forward.

'I was on duty the night the air war started. We had been listening to "Baghdad Betty" on the radio and suddenly she went off the air, so we turned on CNN and got the first reports from journalists in Baghdad that the bombing had started. I ran down and woke up Lt Col Herman, telling him the war had begun. We had prepared for this, having divided the unit up into four-man teams. We stuck with these same teams throughout the campaign, although we also had a sub-group for a section mission that required just two jets.

'This arrangement worked well, as you never had to worry about learning how to brief and fly with a new guy on a combat mission. I flew with Maj Wade "Dog" Straw. We would review our sortie plan and help each other get into our flight gear and put on our sidearms. We swapped the lead and wingman roles on each mission. No long brief was required, except for the target area brief, as we flew together so often and knew standard operating procedures.'

Capt Greg Bogard flew in VMA-542's first *Desert Storm* mission;

'I was in the first division as "Dash 4". "Mongoose" (Lt Col Herman) was the lead, with "Vapor" (Capt Walsh) as "Dash 2" and "Lovey" (Lt Col Lovejoy) as "Dash 3". We were on alert, and launched in response to Iraqi artillery shelling the town of Khafji. We flew over a scattered/broken cloud layer with ceilings at around 7000 ft. An OV-10 from VMO-2 was our FAC(A). He was in the target area describing the target to us. I remember feeling pretty safe as I thought that if a Bronco could orbit near the target then the threat had to be low.

'We crossed the coastline into the target area at about 8000 ft. The OV-10 marked the artillery position with WP (white phosphorus) rockets and all four jets came across the target with about ten to fifteen seconds separation. "Dash 1" and "Dash 2" dropped four Mk 83s and Lovey and I dropped four Mk 20s. We came off, and then all four of us made strafing passes on individual revetments as instructed by the FAC(A). At the end of it all, I had made five runs on the same target, which is pretty stupid in retrospect. However, all four of us came home, and confirmed four of six artillery tubes destroyed. I remember the troops lining the runway and cheering us on as we taxied to de-arm. We were the first VMA-542 pilots to have seen combat since Vietnam.'

The air war lasted from 17 January to 28 February 1991 and AV-8Bs saw action on every day of the conflict. Harrier II pilots flew missions as prescribed by the CENTAF-developed ATO. Most sorties in the battlefield preparation phase (17 January to 22 February) were battlefield air interdiction (BAI) missions designed to attrite Iraqi artillery and other defences (tanks, entrenched infantry, command posts and logistics centres) in Kuwait, thus reducing their ability to defend the KTO once the Coalition launched its ground offensive.

A section of AV-8Bs would take off at a designated time and, if not assigned a confirmed mission on the ATO, arrive on station over Kuwait. Here, they would check in with an F/A-18D FastFAC or OV-10 FAC(A) – the latter started operating off the coast after two Broncos were shot down by shoulder-launched SAMs in the KTO. If not needed to immediately support ground forces as part of the 'push CAS' system, the AV-8B pilots would check in with a FAC and he would assign them to hit specific targets (typically Iraqi artillery or vehicles) or tell them to fly armed reconnaissance in a kill box. They were cleared to hit any targets they could identify within the latter. Kill boxes were initially 30 x 30-mile areas, but they were later divided into 15 x 15-mile squares, identified on a gridded map by alphanumeric designators.

'To get a proper view of our area of operations in Kuwait, one must visualise a small country, not a large American state', recalled Lt Col Herman. 'Southeastern Kuwait was our area of operations, approximately 35 x 70 miles in size. One could see the east coast from the western border. All of our targets were accessible within a ten-minute run – usually less – from the farthest border. We spoke of areas in nicknames, such as the "Army Barracks", the "Golf Course" and the "Pentagon", all of which were easily recognisable from the air. Within that small area there were more than 12 Iraqi divisions.

'By transiting at high altitude – 20,000-30,000 ft, depending on the weather – and employing high dives, we negated most of the Iraqi AAA

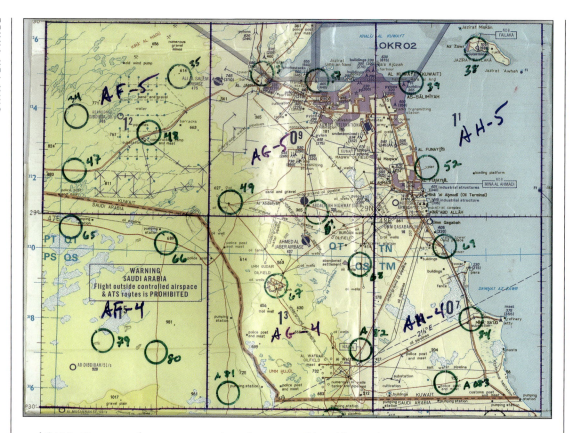

and SAMs. But to see the targets properly and guarantee hits without wasting ordnance, we went to lower altitudes for our Mk 20 Rockeye II CBUs. This, and poor weather, necessarily pulled the AV-8Bs down to within range of some of the hostile fire.

'VMA-311 lost a jet on 28 January followed by VMA-231 on 9 February, their pilots, Capts Michael Berryman and Russell Sanborn, being captured by the Iraqis – we did not know this at the time, however. On the night of 23 February, one of my pilots, Capt James N "Trey" Wilbourne, was killed while attacking a gathering point for tanks. Two days later, the jet of squadronmate Capt Scott "Vapor" Walsh took a hit from a hand-held SAM, but he managed to nurse his aeroplane back to friendly territory before safely ejecting. Walsh was flying missions once again just four days later. The final loss to enemy action came on 27 February when a VMA-331 aircraft flown by Capt Reginald Underwood was brought down, resulting in the death of the pilot.

'These final losses came once the ground war had commenced, when pilots were pushing harder for targets as our "grunts" crossed the border into Kuwait. Thirty-six days of air preparation allowed the mechanised troops to rapidly advance into the KTO. We pushed hard, realising that two-thirds of the Marine Corps was on the ground driving into 12 Iraqi divisions.

'I had my own close encounter with an IR SAM early on in the conflict when my division was flying only its second mission of *Desert Storm*. We were working with a ground FAC near the eastern edge of Kuwait, right on the border. As we rolled in on some trench lines, my wingman

The map of southern Kuwait, showing kill boxes and navigation waypoints, that Lt Col Herman used throughout the campaign. 'Southeast Kuwait, our primary area of operations, was approximately 35 by 70 miles in area', Herman explained. 'Within that small area there were more than 12 Iraqi divisions. By transiting at high altitude – 20,000-30,000 ft – and employing high dives, we negated most of the Iraqi AAA and SAMs. But to see the targets and guarantee hits without wasting ordnance, we descended to lower altitudes with our Mk 20 Rockeye IIs. This, and heavy weather, pulled the AV-8Bs down to within range of the enemy's hostile fire' (*Ted Herman*)

VMA-542's RAF exchange pilot Sqn Ldr Andy Dakin (left) poses with Capt James N 'Trey' Wilbourne in front of 'Tiger 05' at King Abdul Aziz pre-war. The latter would lose his life during a night bombing attack against troop emplacements just north of Ali Al Salem airfield, in the KTO, on 23 February 1991 (*Ted Herman*)

"Vapor" (Capt Scott Walsh) called "off target" without dropping. Just as I was about to drop, my HUD attack symbology went away, so I too started to pull out. Suddenly, an SA-7 shot by my nose with a monstrous smoke trail. I yelled at "Vapor" to break right and to pop flares, since it was now obvious it was going after him! My left hand was stroking the flare switch like crazy too! Laden with six Rockeye IIs, his aeroplane and mine struggled for altitude. It seemed like 30 minutes had passed before we got to 10,000 ft and the missile had fallen off behind us.

'Capt Will Hettinger, "Dash Four" in our flight, saw the launch point of the missile and laid four 1000-lb bombs right on top of the position. That ruined the gunner's day.

'Typically, no one saw IR man-portable missiles being launched, and that remained a problem both for us and the other aviation communities throughout the war.'

Col Tomassetti commented on the AV-8B's need to bomb from lower altitudes during *Desert Storm*, which in turn made the Harrier II vulnerable to IR SAMs;

'From high altitude you can employ weapons with a relative sanctuary from the threat, but spotting and identifying targets is a bigger challenge. With the sensors we had at the time – the ARBS TV camera with a small magnification – this was a bit of a problem. The ARBS was a point sensor. It was not good at broadly searching an area and then zooming in on a point target. You had to know where to look, focus in on the general direction of the potential target and then focus on the target within the ARBS's field of view.

'We got used to high-angle deliveries of slick Mk 82 bombs from higher altitudes, with a release at around 8000 ft. When you rolled in at higher altitudes you could usually get a good lock on against a target at around 10,000-12,000 ft. At those heights you might be able to determine a tank from an armoured personnel carrier or a truck, but you could not tell what specific model of vehicle it was. So, using these higher altitude tactics, you became very reliant on the FastFACs and FAC(A)s being able to spot and confirm targets. They could stay around the target area using their superior sensors such as a FLIR and binoculars, employed by the back-seater, to determine targets. As long as the FAC gave us a good mark, we felt pretty certain that we would hit the target.

'Our three primary weapons loads were six Mk 82s (usually slick), four 1000-lb Mk 83s or six Mk 20 Rockeye IIs. We carried AIM-9M Sidewinders on the outboard stations for the first week or so, but when it seemed there was little possibility of meeting up with Iraqi fighters we downloaded the missiles and used the outboard stations for more air-to-ground weapons.

'We always carried the 25 mm cannon, and I used it a lot on BAI missions, usually shooting all 300 rounds. The gun was good for suppressing AAA. When the first guy in a section rolled in, he fired his cannon to silence the gunners so the wingman could attack unimpeded by AAA. It was a good suppression weapon to get the guys on the ground to put their heads down, even if it was not really that accurate when fired from medium altitude. Often, we would roll in, fire 100 or so rounds from the gun and then drop our bombs. If it was too much to do both, the lead pilot would fire his gun and then come around again and expend his bombs after "Dash Two" had dropped his.

'Harrier II units focused mostly on targets in Kuwait, although a small number of missions were also flown over southern Iraq. The enemy had moved so much military equipment and troops into the KTO that there were more targets than we could have ever possibly hit. It got to the point that you could recognise Iraqi positions from the air pretty easily. They tended to set up their AAA positions and artillery batteries in similar patterns, so when you flew over them you knew what you were looking at simply by recognising the wheel track patterns in the sand. You could also spot where the sand had been disturbed when making trenches and bunkers. By the second week of the air war, we were pretty skilled at identifying what we saw below us, which in turn meant that we could pick out defensive positions and targets.

'We had a Landsat photo of southern Kuwait, as well as detailed maps. Our intel folks also gave us a good indication of what Iraqi units were where, and how we might attack them – we had a pretty good idea of the Iraqi order of battle. All of this information was rather basic compared to what we have today when we go into battle, however.

'Looking back, we gave the Iraqis a lot more credit than they probably deserved. It turned out that their air defences were not nearly as coordinated as we thought they would be. Their systems were neither as reliable nor as effective as expected. But what they did have was a lot of AAA, and they used it extensively. They had no qualms about sending as many bullets into the air as they possibly could. This was not a bad tactic if you were trying to keep aeroplanes away, or at higher altitudes.

'For two days right before the ground war, we dropped Mk 77 napalm bombs. This was not something you did from high altitude. You had to drop them from low altitude at a low angle so as to get a nice stretch of fire on the ground. We were well below 3000 ft on our approach to the target, and I could see people on the ground firing at me with small arms. This was a bit unnerving, and I am glad that we did not fly these low altitude strikes for very long. Our goal was to burn off the oil-filled trenches before our forces got to these positions. We did not lose any aircraft during the napalm strikes, despite these sorties being about the riskiest missions we flew in the Harrier II during *Desert Storm*.'

From 28 January to 1 February VMA-542 and other AV-8B units completed more than 90 BAI missions in support of the Battle of Khafji. During the following week the squadron flew mostly day BAI sorties against defensive positions manned by the 14th and 18th Infantry Divisions and the 5th Mechanised Division in southern Kuwait. One such mission was undertaken by Capt Scott Walsh on 4 February, and his combat report read as follows;

'"Combat 41" (F/A-18D FAC(A)) found an armoured column just off the northeast/southwest road about seven miles northeast of the Al Wafra oilfield. The XO (Lt Col Kevin Leffler) and "Sal" (Capt Salathe) had just dropped on it, with mixed results. The FAC(A) marked the target with a WP rocket and popped flares. As I rolled in behind "Beav" (Capt Bogard), the road to the south lit up with AAA. I called the AAA to "Beav" as he pickled his ordnance – his six Mk 20 canisters opened up right down the road on top of the AAA muzzle flashes.

'I then lined up on the vehicles and dropped my six Mk 20 CBUs on the armoured column. The FAC(A) reported that the bomb pattern went through the middle of the column. We were getting secondary explosions, and he gave us a BDA (bomb damage assessment) of "50/50" – 50 percent of bombs on target, destroying 50 percent of the target. I figured "Beav" took out three to four AAA weapons and their personnel. Maj Gen Robert Johnson's brief that night on CNN said that four Harrier IIs had destroyed 20-25 tanks.'

In mid-February VMA-542 flew an average of 32 sorties per day. The principal focus of battlefield shaping attacks during this period were artillery and tank positions in west central Kuwait, this weaponry being operated by the 7th and 8th Infantry Divisions. Amongst the pilots to see action against enemy tanks at this time was Capt Mike 'Disco' Beguelin, as detailed in his 17 February combat report;

'During a morning patrol just south of Um Gudair oilfield, a FastFAC found six tanks hidden in old bomb craters. The ceiling was around 8000 ft, and we came in low under the clouds from the east soon after the FAC put a marking rocket on the target. "Rebel" (Maj Jim Lee) and I rolled in almost simultaneously from combat spread, with me on the outside. We dropped 12 Rockeye II CBUs on the tanks and egressed to the west. Four of the tanks were completely covered by bomblets, with very good effects on the targets. Target time was about 0715 hrs.'

Battlefield prep missions intensified in the third week of February, and from the 20th to the 23rd AV-8B squadrons flew strikes against Iraqi defences in areas of the KTO through which I MEF and pan-Arab forces would launch their offensive – VMA-542 pilots surged to fly 58 sorties on the 22nd. Forty-eight hours later the ground war finally commenced, despite poor weather conditions blanketing southern Kuwait in low cloud. Between 24 and 28 February all Harrier II pilots flew an intensive series of CAS and BAI sorties to pave the way for the mechanised troops, targeting Iraqi forces that were found to be in a position to stall the Coalition advance.

'Just before the ground war commenced we received information from Division on how it was going to play out', explained Col Tomasetti. 'Our primary mission during the ground war phase was to take out stuff that was going to cause a problem for the advancing troops. Artillery was a primary threat, followed by tanks. We were also tasked with the destruction of battlefield obstacles. We flew a mix of BAI, which usually entailed going to a 30-by-30-mile square kill box, armed reconnaissance and CAS – the latter had to be performed under the guidance of a FAC. For me personally, my missions were evenly split between working CAS with a FAC and carrying out BAI/armed recce. Sometimes we cancelled missions due to weather – it rained a lot in the winter – and occasionally we came back with bombs still on due to a lack of targets or fuel exhaustion while waiting for the FAC to guide us.'

Capt Scott Walsh found himself in the thick of the action on 24 February as Coalition forces penetrated the Kuwaiti border and drove north;

'"Salt" (Maj Peters) and I were proceeding to grid reference B-10 on our second mission of the day when we heard FAC(A) "Combat 53" call a priority mission for any "Jump" (the AV-8B call-sign of the day) flight jets. The FAC(A) said he had an active artillery battery with people running around. Another "Jump" flight responded first, and we came in two minutes later and made three passes each, dropping a total of 12 Mk 20 CBUs and shooting more than 200 cannon rounds at the battery. I saw "Salt" get secondary explosions out of two revetments, and the whole battery was suppressed or destroyed through the combined firepower of the two "Jump" flights.

'This mission was significant because we were doing exactly what MEF planners had wanted us to do – suppress the artillery while the "grunts" were moving through the breach. This attack was made in the late afternoon, and I believe 1st MARDIV was going through the second breach at this time.'

Maj Gen J M Myatt, Commanding General of 1st MARDIV, relied on pilots such as Capt Walsh both in the lead up to the ground offensive and once his troops had entered the KTO;

'The pilots become so familiar with what I call the I MEF zone of action after they had been flying over it for three weeks that they were able to sit down with my commanders and talk about what they had seen, and what we were going to face. I recall that Maj Gen Moore sent a couple of Harrier II guys out to brief us, as they had been flying in direct support of 1st MARDIV since the very start of the conflict. There was no substitute for the pilots actually coming down and talking to my folks.

'We knew that 700 Iraqi artillery pieces could range us as we went through the obstacle belt. Gen Moore instructed his F/A-18D FastFACs on what to do on the Quick Fire radio channel if we took incoming artillery rounds. Our TPQ-35 counter-battery radars, set to locate the artillery firing positions, were linked directly with the FastFACs, who in turn directed attack aircraft against them. Between 0600 hrs and 1400 hrs on 24 February, we had 42 instances of incoming artillery that we handled this way. We were able to use our artillery to attack 24 of the 42 targets. The remainder were attacked by Marine AV-8Bs within a few minutes of the artillery fire being detected. I am very proud of our air-ground coordination.'

A close up of 'personalised' Mk 20 Rockeye II CBUs attached to the wing pylons of VMA-542 AV-8B BuNo 162945. These weapons proved extremely effective throughout *Desert Storm*, with 'Tigers'' pilot Capt Mike Beguelin using them to deadly effect on the morning of 17 February. 'A FAC found six tanks hidden in old bomb craters. We came in low under the clouds from the east, and the FAC put a marking rocket on the target. "Rebel" (Maj Jim Lee) and I rolled in and we dropped 12 Rockeye II cluster bombs on the tanks. Four of them were completely covered by bomblets, with very good effects on the targets' (*Ted Herman*)

In February VMA-542 flew 786 combat sorties for a total of 930 combat hours, with a 92.4 percent mission capable rate. Pilots expended 2735 Mk 20s, 480 Mk 82s, 160 Mk 77 napalm canisters, 61 Mk 83s and four AGM-65E Maverick missiles. They also fired 14,826 rounds of 25 mm cannon ammunition.

'As a result of our extensive defence suppression attacks at the start of the air war, it was rare that we heard SA-2 or SA-3 alerts on our electronic countermeasures systems during these late war missions', Col Tomassetti recalled. 'This was because it soon became apparent to Iraqi radar operators that when they turned on their tracking equipment we would destroy it with either a HARM anti-radar missile or some other weapon. After the first few days of the conflict the Iraqis chose not to turn on their radars much at all. We heard occasional AAA and SAM beeps, but then they quickly turned them off. The biggest threats we faced were the 57 mm S-60 AAA pieces, 23 mm ZSU-23-4 batteries and shoulder-launched IR SAMs. If we put our jets in the low/medium altitude environment, where these weapons could be effective, we ran the risk of being shot down. Where they had AAA, they had lots of it. It was usually easy to spot, however, as you could see the tracers both day and night.

'Over the course of the air war we refined our tactics. Initially, our squadron concept was to deploy chaff and flares pre-emptively as we rolled into the target and then climbed back out again after dropping our ordnance. This was stopped when we discovered early on in the air war that the AV-8B was proving hard to spot from the ground because of its small size and grey camouflage, combined with the aggressive

A photograph taken through the AV-8B's Smiths Industries HUD on approach to King Abdul Aziz. 'When I fought in *Desert Storm* I thought the AV-8B was the greatest thing flying', stated Col Tomassetti. 'It had a good HUD, it had a multi-purpose display in the cockpit and it had HOTAS for quick and efficient weapons and sensor selection. It was a great aeroplane to fly for both the attack mission and CAS' (*'Rusty' Jones*)

evasive manoeuvres that we were flying at medium altitude. We knew that the jet was hard to detect when our ground FACs complained that they were having a hard time spotting us, despite them knowing where to look as we came towards them. It was even harder for the enemy, who had no idea where to look when we were attacking from higher altitudes.

'Even if we didn't deploy flares, enemy gunners usually worked out where we were after the first aircraft in the section had rolled in and dropped its weapons. The second aircraft would then invariably get shot at, for the Iraqis would target the area where the noise of the first jet had come from. We quickly reacted to this by approaching the target from different directions. The Iraqis also had a habit of shooting in the general area of our flares, so we started using these only when we came off a hot target where we were at a low enough altitude to be at risk from SAMs and radar-guided AAA, or if there was a known threat in the area according to our intel folks.

'However, if there was no indication that the Iraqi gunners knew that we were there – our attacks had not provoked a response from AAA batteries – then we would drop bombs and not use flares or chaff. If we had to make a second run, then we would try and use flares to keep ourselves safe, plus come in from a different heading.

'We were getting re-supplied with weapons about every other day, so our ordnance load-out depended on both availability and projected targets. If we knew that we were going against artillery or vehicles, we usually carried Mk 20 Rockeye II CBUs. For strikes against AAA sites, hardened bunkers or similar targets, we used Mk 82 500-lb or, if available, Mk 83 1000-lb bombs.'

During *Desert Storm* more than 90 percent of the AV-8B sorties flown were BAI and armed reconnaissance missions, and only about five percent involved CAS – these were all flown during the Khafji battles and the ground invasion. When the ground assault finally came, I MEF, Saudi and pan-Arab forces recaptured Kuwait, while the bulk of the US Army, British and French forces pushed into Iraq via the 'great left hook' and crushed Saddam's forces west and north of Kuwait with massive air support.

Lt Col Ted Herman summed up his squadron's contribution to the war as follows;

'The Harrier IIs of VMA-542 ultimately flew 1037 combat sorties, totalling 1240 combat hours, in just 43 days. We dropped just over two million pounds of ordnance and fired 15,000 rounds of 25 mm ammunition. It was a proud day for me on 17 January 1991 when I carried our "Tiger" flag over Kuwait on the first VMA-542 mission since the Vietnam War. I was even prouder on 28 February 1991 when I flew the squadron's last sortie of the war knowing that we had witnessed an historic 43 days of combat, and added another chapter to the illustrious history of the Marine Corps and VMA-542 "Tigers".'

Pilots and senior support personnel of VMA-542 'Tigers' pose for an October 1990 group photograph. These men flew 1037 combat sorties and delivered more than two million pounds of ordnance during *Desert Storm* (*Ted Herman*)

VMA-331 AND VMA-513

On 7 August 1990 the 13th Marine Expeditionary Unit/Special Missions Capable (MEU/SOC), already deployed aboard ships of the Seventh Fleet Amphibious Ready Group (ARG) in the western Pacific, was ordered to prepare to move to the Arabian Gulf. The same day, 4th MEB was told to prepare for deployment in support of *Desert Shield*.

The Marine Corps always deploy with a mix of ground combat, command, support and air power to form a combined arms task force. One of the reasons 4th MEB was selected for this assignment was it had trained for, and was preparing to support, NATO Exercise *Teamwork/Bold Guard 90* in Europe. Multiple units were rapidly assigned to augment and fill out 4th MEB for this deployment. MAG-40, under the command of Col Glenn F Burgess, was the air combat element for 4th MEB, the group including five helicopter squadrons and associated support, logistics, command and air defence units, as well as AV-8B squadron VMA-331 for CAS.

In 1990, the US Navy had a force of about 60 amphibious ships divided into three ARGs and eleven squadrons to provide worldwide lift for the Marine Corps and to undertake contingency operations. At any one time, at least two three- to five-ship ARGs, with attached MEUs, were forward deployed – ARG Alpha operated in the western Pacific and ARG Bravo in the Mediterranean.

Amphibious vessels included aircraft carrier-size *Tarawa* and *Iwo Jima* class ships, *Austin*, *Raleigh* and *Anchorage* class dock landing ships, *Newport* class tank landing ships and cargo vessels configured for rapid unloading such as the *Charleston* class. For an amphibious assault or beach landing, specialised vessels ranging from helicopters to Landing Craft Air Cushion hovercraft and Landing Craft Utilities were needed to bring tanks, artillery, men and materiel rapidly ashore.

The US Navy's ARG 2, led by Rear Adm John B LaPlante, was assigned the task of moving 4th MEB to the Middle East. The US Navy was short of ships to transport forces committed to *Desert Shield*. Indeed, only 13 amphibious vessels could be identified for ARG 2 to move 4th MEB when 20 to 24 ships were needed. Men and materiel critical to the operation had to be placed on Military Sealift Command ships not configured for amphibious work – these were civilian manned and leased.

A major challenge for 4th MEB, MAG-40 and other command and support elements of the force was the rapid reconfiguration from a group planned to support a NATO exercise into one prepared to fight a war in the Middle East, with little time and less than optimum transportation arrangements. The amount of time available to load up the ships and the space limitations on the available transport were to significantly impact on the ability of 4th MEB's ground and air components to perform their assigned missions off the coast of Kuwait and Saudi Arabia. For example, *Nassau* was designated as the flagship of the amphibious force. It carried a major part of the command element of 4th MEB, but the ship was also 'stuffed' with 20 AV-8Bs and three AH-1W Sea Cobras and six UH-1N Huey helicopters, as well as support equipment, medical teams, maintenance personnel and troops.

VMA-331, the primary fixed-wing element assigned to MAG-40, could trace its history back to 1943, when it was formed as a scout-bomber squadron. The unit saw plenty of action in the Pacific, but was deactivated following the end of World War 2. Reactivated in 1954 and equipped with the AD Skyraider, the 'Bumblebees' transitioned to the A4D Skyhawk in 1958 and subsequently flew five extended deployments to Vietnam with the fighter-bomber. In 1985, VMA-331 became the first to convert to the AV-8B, operating from Cherry Point. It trained for shipboard operations from 1986, and embarked the first six-aircraft Harrier II detachment aboard USS *Belleau Wood* (LHA-3) in early 1987.

By 1990 VMA-331 was led by Lt Col J W Fitzgerald, who reported;

'During the first week of August, VMA-331 was participating in Type Commanders Amphibious training aboard USS *Iwo Jima* (LPH-2), attempting to complete work-ups in preparation for a squadron deployment in support of 4th MEB for the *Teamwork 90* exercise. The invasion of Kuwait by Iraq on 2 August resulted in an early termination of the exercise for the "Bumblebees". Contingency planning by CENTCOM and CINCLANT resulted in a warning order for the squadron to deploy 20 aircraft aboard *Nassau* by 20 August.

USS *Nassau* (LHA-4) conducts final preparations off the coast of North Carolina prior to departing for the Middle East. Six newly repainted AV-8Bs from VMA-331 can be seen ranged forward on the vessel's flightdeck, a further 14 Harrier IIs being chained down on the stern of the vessel. Aside from the AV-8Bs, LHA-4 also embarked three AH-1W Sea Cobras and six UH-1N Hueys from HMLA-269. *Nassau* departed the USA on 20 August 1990 and stayed in the Arabian Gulf region until 20 April 1991 (*US Navy*)

On 22 November 1990, President George H W Bush visited LHA-4 to thank the vessel's US Navy and Marine Corps team for their ongoing service and support during Operation *Desert Shield*. Behind the President can be seen AV-8Bs, UH-1Ns and a solitary AH-1W (*US Navy*)

'The AV-8B had been conducting shipboard deployments and exercises as early as 1986. However, the plan for *Desert Shield* afforded the first opportunity for an entire squadron to be embarked aboard an LHA. A similar experience was when 20 AV-8As were deployed aboard *Nassau* on 8 April 1981. The chief differences, aside from the two completely different V/STOL aircraft, were the intentions to simultaneously embark helicopter assets while making *Nassau* the chief staff vessel of the amphibious task force. These two differences necessitated large operational compromises on the part of VMA-331.'

There was a massive amount of work to do to change from a ten-aircraft training mission to a full squadron wartime plan. VMA-331 had to add 11 pilots, two ground officers, 19 senior NCOs and 105 enlisted personnel to its ranks just a week before the planned deployment date of 15 August! New pilots assigned to the unit busily worked through a quick training programme, with the support of VMAT-203, to qualify all pilots for shipboard operations. Meanwhile, squadron support personnel focused on packing the correct mix of maintenance equipment, spare

An AV-8B returns to VMA-331 following a training mission from LHA-4 whilst the vessel was en route to the Arabian Gulf. The two aircraft parked in the foreground are being refuelled after recent sorties. When operating from an LHA AV-8B pilots would perform a short take-off followed by a vertical landing, the latter phase of the mission being relatively easy during daylight hours but a significant challenge at night or in reduced visibility. In order to achieve successful flight operations from LHA-4, VMA-311 personnel, ship's crew and the ARG's command team had to work closely together. This was not always an easy task (*US Navy*)

parts and other material that would be needed to keep a squadron of Harrier IIs combat capable whilst at sea.

All VMA-331 aircraft had their green paint and leading edges sprayed over with grey and their air intakes painted white to make them blend in better with the Middle East environment. Flight tests subsequently showed that this new camouflage made the jets much harder to spot, especially when operating at medium altitudes.

Maj (later Col) Ben Hancock was one of the 11 pilots sent to bolster VMA-331's ranks;

'I was an instructor pilot with VMAT-203 at Cherry Point when the Iraqis invaded Kuwait. I was on leave in Flagstaff, Arizona, and called back to my squadron to see if I needed to come back early. I was told to enjoy the rest of my leave. The next morning the admin officer called and told me to get back to Cherry Point that night! I tried to find out what was going on, but he could not tell me a thing. I hung up the phone and then told my wife Jan that we had to get back immediately, but I did not know exactly why. She called another Marine's wife, and within five minutes she told me I had a FCLP (field carrier landing practice) period scheduled for the next morning, and that I was sailing aboard *Nassau* with VMA-331 to the Arabian Gulf. Again, the wives intel network was ahead of the game.

'I flew back to Cherry Point, did two passes in a jet lightly loaded with fuel to one of the Harrier pads and was blessed as "carrier qualified". A few days later, I flew an AV-8B with four drop tanks out onto *Nassau*. I had not flown a jet off a ship for two years, but there I was.'

Aircraft flew aboard *Nassau* on 18-19 August, and the four-ship task force left for the Middle East on the 20th. Flying commenced that same day, with the goal of completing pilot certifications for shipboard operations and integrating the vessel with the embarked squadrons. On 30 August the task force sailed into the Mediterranean Sea. Training was expanded to include air intercept, weapons and low-level operations.

Flying in the high temperatures of the Middle East called for careful management of the AV-8B around the ship. This limited Harrier II weapons loads to four Mk 82s, four Mk 20s or two Mk 83s, and no gun was fitted until the weather got cooler.

In transit, the Marines of 4th MEB, MAG-40 and two other smaller amphibious groups – 13th MEU (SOC), sailing from the Pacific, and MAGTF 6-90 from Okinawa – were still in the dark about their role in *Desert Shield*. At this same time, initial elements of 7th MEB were arriving in Saudi Arabia by air, securing equipment landed at Al Jubail Naval Base from MPSs and taking up defensive positions north and west along the coast.

On 31 August CENTCOM released *Desert Shield* Amphibious Operations Order 1-90. This listed the three groups mentioned above as Marine Forces Afloat, and

Chained down Harrier IIs from VMA-331 frame other vessels within *Nassau's* amphibious task force as they cross the Atlantic in August 1990. By January 1991 the US Navy has assembled the largest fleet of amphibious shipping ready for action since a 1964 exercise. This force was held at sea as an operational reserve throughout the conflict following serious debate at the top levels of the US leadership concerning the benefits versus the risks of an Inchon-style assault into Kuwait or southern Iraq (*Ben Hancock*)

designated the 12,000 Marines and associated units embarked in 24 ships to be the theatre reserve. They were to be used only at the direction of Gen Schwarzkopf.

US Navy and Marine Corps staff developed a list of ten options for amphibious operations ranging from an assault against Iraqi forces on or near the Kuwait coast to raids against specific targets to force the Iraqis to deploy additional units to defend the beaches. Low-risk landings to reinforce Coalition ground forces were also evaluated.

On 6 September *Nassau* entered the Suez Canal, and by the 13th the ship was off the coast of Oman. The US Navy and Marine Corps worked together with the Sultanate of Oman to secure approvals to use Omani airspace and beaches for amphibious rehearsal and training exercise *Sea Soldier I*. This was held from 27 September to 3 October, and involved more than 2400 personnel and 390 vehicles, with support from Marine Corps helicopters and AV-8Bs. *Sea Soldier II*, which was a larger-scale amphibious exercise involving 3100 Marines from 4th and 13th MEUs, US Navy aircraft from USS *Independence* (CV-62), Marine aircraft from Bahrain and the AV-8Bs of VMA-331, was held along the coast of Oman from 30 October to 8 November. These exercises gave the 'Bumblebees' the opportunity to demonstrate their surge and CAS capabilities, and also provided access to Omani bombing ranges.

Training continued, and on 15-21 November both 4th MEB and VMA-331 participated in multi-national exercise *Imminent Thunder*. Widely covered by the press, this event again gave the 'Bumblebees' the chance to operate their jets within an integrated air, ground and sea force.

By this point VMA-331 pilots and their support team had trained enough to be able to operate effectively from *Nassau* and fly the mix of naval and amphibious missions projected to both defend the task force and support amphibious operations. The squadron developed a set of operational plans for various potential combat scenarios, and had proved its utility in the *Sea Soldier* exercises.

However, there was considerable friction between the US Navy, amphibious task force commanders and the Marine Corps about the role of *Nassau*. With a load of 20 AV-8Bs and nine helicopters, the vessel could no longer be used as a vertical assault platform. The Marine Corps wanted to keep the AV-8Bs and helicopters on the ship to act as organic aviation support for any future amphibious operations. In addition, there seemed to be no more room at the bases close to the battle zone to accommodate the AV-8Bs.

On the other hand, the US Navy viewed the use of *Nassau* in the 'Harrier Carrier' role as a misuse of limited amphibious shipping. No more than 14 AV-8Bs could operate from its deck at any one time, and the ship only had a sufficient arsenal of weapons to support three days of Harrier II war-surge operations. Also, due to range and targeting challenges, *Nassau* would need to stay in the dangerous waters close to Kuwait in order to support air operations. For all of these reasons the US Navy wanted the jets of VMA-331 to be brought ashore. The Harrier II pilots were also keen to come ashore, as Col Hancock explained;

'Our squadron flew training missions and tried to stay proficient while "stuck" aboard the ship. It seemed like our biggest enemy for much of the time was *Nassau* itself. Although there were hundreds of hard-working

Photographed between training missions in the mid-Atlantic in late August 1990, this aircraft has yet to have the twin gun pods attached to its underfuselage centreline. Note VMA-331's distinctive 'Bumblebee' unit emblem on the nose and, to the left of it, artwork depicting a winged 'Oscar the Grouch' from *Sesame Street*! (*Ben Hancock*)

Pilots from VMA-331 flew regular training missions from *Nassau* during the transatlantic crossing and once in the Arabian Gulf. Armed with a pair of live AIM-9Ms, this aircraft was photographed conducting just such a mission off the Saudi Arabian coast during *Desert Shield* (*Ben Hancock*)

Navy officers and sailors on the ship who bent over backwards to assist the embarked Marines in their missions, we fought pitched battles with some of them while trying to keep our jets and pilots 100 percent prepared for combat. We were constantly cancelling flight ops to conduct RAS FAS (replenishment at sea and refuelling at sea), unrep and vertrep (underway and vertical replenishment at sea).

'The bulk of the Navy officers onboard seemed to be doctors, dentists and supply officers. Whereas the Navy carrier air wings onboard the large "flattops" were the "tip of the spear", where they wanted to be, the LHA/LPH "Gator Navy" seemed to be content holding up the rear and doing "gator squares" – steaming around in circles hundreds of miles away from the threat.'

Following the *Sea Soldier III* exercise in early December, 4th MEB leadership called for more night training, as Col Hancock recalled;

'In mid-December the Commanding General of 4th MEB, Maj Gen Harry W Jenkins Jr, decided that he needed to have fixed-wing CAS available at night. So, even though none of us had flown a single night sortie in four months, we were given a short lecture on night ops and launched off the pointy end of the ship. The first couple of passes were under "pinky" conditions at dusk, which was nice since you could "cheat" and see the ship in the low light. All of a sudden the curtain went down and now you were out there in the black night trying to find the back end of your ship among the 20-odd vessels of the task force.

'Once you were down to vertical landing weight by either burning or dumping fuel to "Charlie" fuel state, you were committed to getting back aboard *Nassau*. Unlike jets operating off a conventional carrier, we did not have any airborne refuelling aircraft to help out. Once you were down to the fuel weight required to land vertically, you did not have enough gas to divert to an airfield ashore.'

In November, the Pentagon decided that more forces were needed to confront the Iraqis. 5th MEB with 7500 troops, along with MAG-50 and support forces, was alerted for deployment. This force left San Diego embarked in 13 ships starting on 1 December. 13th MEU, which had been allowed to return to the Pacific in November, was called on to return to the Middle East too. When 5th MEB arrived in the Arabian Sea, and 13th MEU returned and met up with 4th MEU on 13 January 1991, together they formed the largest Marine Forces Afloat since 1964. This massive force created command, control and sustainment challenges.

The UN deadline passed on 15 January, and on the night of the 17th the air assault began with strikes on targets throughout Iraq. 4th and 5th MEBs, however, stayed out of the action for the time being. Six days after *Desert Storm* commenced, the brigades conducted Exercise *Sea Soldier IV* along the coast of Oman from 23 January to 4 February as a rehearsal for a possible amphibious assault.

However, there was still a debate about how the massive amphibious force would be employed. Despite heavy lobbying for an operation likened to Inchon in the Korean War by many senior officers, especially the Marine Corps Commandant Gen A M 'Al' Gray, the Marine Forces Afloat continued to remain in reserve. The initial plan for the assault into Kuwait, which included a one corps attack with 4th MEB in support, had been reviewed by the US leadership in October and assessed as being too risky. A two corps plan with various amphibious assault options targeting Kuwait or the Al Faw region of Iraq, was also reviewed. However, computer war game simulations pointed out many challenges with the amphibious options, including heavy Iraqi defences leading to unacceptable casualties, the risk of mines and the impact of poor weather.

The Iraqis had elements from four infantry divisions located along the coast, and they had built strong defences supported by minefields and beach obstacles. Off the coast, the waters were filled with ten minefields, and 'Silkworm' anti-ship missile batteries had been moved into the area.

The lack of a decision on how best to use the amphibious force had an adverse affect on the morale of VMA-331, as Col Hancock explained;

'*Desert Storm* started without VMA-331 and *Nassau*. The amphibious task force's mission wasn't really clear yet, and we were being held out for a possible amphibious assault, or to act as reserves. Our sister Harrier II squadrons in Saudi Arabia had been involved from Day One.

Four VMA-331 aircraft armed with Mk 83 1000-lb bombs prepare to launch from *Nassau* during a training exercise in the Arabian Gulf during *Desert Shield* (*Peter Mersky collection*)

'To me it was very disheartening to be sitting in the ready room eating popcorn and watching the ship's movie while reading about my fellow Marines getting shot at. We were constantly being told that we would start flying combat missions any day now, but they were just as constantly being delayed. We would be told to prepare to fly into combat the next day, so we would spend all night doing mission planning, only to be cancelled the next morning.

'The worst part of this period was that one of our squadron pilots was killed on a night training mission while trying to get back aboard the ship. Capt Manny "Buick" Rivera died on 22 January about three miles behind *Nassau* – the ship was anchored just off the beach. We were flying modified tactical air navigation systems approaches because the ship's radar system, used for guiding pilots in on precision Carrier-Controlled Approaches, had been "down" for most of the cruise.'

The pilots of VMA-331 flew 2838 sorties totalling 2426 hours of training time in the nearly seven months the unit operated off *Nassau*. These impressive statistics were due exclusively to the outstanding effort made by the squadron's support team during this intense training period, which ran from 18 August 1990 until late February 1991.

Col Hancock continued;

'January passed and still we weren't in the fight. By now Gen Jenkins was getting impatient, and he started pressing the Navy pretty hard to sail further north so that VMA-331 and HMLA-269 could get close enough to conduct combat operations if necessary. Some of us believed that while we were awake the ship would sail north, and then while we slept it would turn around and head back south toward safer waters!

'On 18 February the helicopter carrier USS *Tripoli* (LPH-10) and the cruiser USS *Princeton* (CG-59) both hit Iraqi mines when sailing within ten miles of each other. At this point it became pretty clear that the amphibious task force was going to be limited in its scope of operations. Indeed, I thought that we would sit out the entire conflict, but Gen Jenkins, who was well liked and respected by all of us, managed to get VMA-331 into the war.'

Finally, on 20 February 1991, VMA-331 launched four AV-8Bs into action. This was the first time that Marine Corps Harriers had been sent into combat from an amphibious assault ship.

'The very first mission was flown by "Mystic" (Lt Col Fitzgerald), "Woody" (Capt Gregory Underwood), "Peewee" (Capt Kevin Hermann) and myself', recalled Col Hancock. 'The ship was located in the middle of the Arabian Gulf about 70 miles due east of the Kuwait border. We had been told the night before to expect to launch for the real thing, but I went to sleep thinking again it would be cancelled. We were woken at about 0300 hrs and told that we were definitely going. We briefed and then launched at 0540 hrs for a dawn strike on Iraqi AAA positions on Failaka Island.

'It was pitch black, there was an 800 ft overcast and it was raining. The flightdeck was crowded with well-wishers and spectators. My first jet broke in the chocks, so ten minutes before take-off I ran to the spare jet. We were carrying 500-lb Mk 82 conical fin high explosive bombs. We each had two AIM-9M Sidewinder missiles and 300 25 mm rounds for our guns. "Woody" was launching without the gun pack, however, carrying an AN/ALQ-164 DECM pod on the centreline station. We also had 40 decoy flares and 20 chaff bundles. We did not have a clue as to what we were about to do, however.

'We launched into the low weather and each of us headed to a pre-briefed rendezvous point. The weather was horrible. We saw two F/A-18s and a few A-6s all crowded into the same small hole as they tried to stay clear of the clouds. We went through all the appropriate Navy and Marine Corps command-and-control wickets and found that no one had any idea as to who we were. VMA-331 was not on the common ATO and had not been scheduled by the boys running the air show in Saudi. They probably did not know we existed until that point. So we just checked in on the radio nets using frequencies we had borrowed from one of the carriers and squawking the proper codes. We used our peacetime call-sign of "Magic" and pretended to know what we were doing, and everybody simply cleared us north. We were in there!

'Well, Failaka Island was socked in, so we did what any good Marine would do. We went further north to our secondary target on Bubiyan Island. Intel had pinpointed artillery just west of the island in northern Kuwait. The clouds were solid as far as we could see. We were going to run in at 37,000 ft and release our bombs through the overcast using our INS waypoints. Maybe we'd get lucky and actually hit something. In any event we didn't want to bring our bombs back to the ship.

'Just north of Kuwait City, "Woody" and I picked up some indications of Iraqi radar systems looking at us. We were now within about three-quarters of a mile of each other when something very big flew out of the clouds and blew up right in the middle of all of us. "Woody" yelled out "They are shooting at us!" It was most likely an SA-2 SAM, and it was a lucky shot by the Iraqis. Nobody got fragged. By now we were only six miles from our target, so we pressed on. We released using the jet's computer system, and I did my best 4G turn. We then ran like hell back to the ship. When we returned to *Nassau* morale was sky high.'

Only 19 of the scheduled VMA-331 sorties planned for 20 February went ahead due to poor weather, but the 'Bumblebees' were finally in the war nevertheless. From then on the efforts of VMA-331 were integrated with the ATO, the unit flying as many missions as possible against Iraqi positions on the occupied Kuwaiti islands of Bubiyan and Failaka so as to convince the enemy that they were supporting an impending amphibious assault. On 21 February the squadron scheduled 44 sorties, but only 26 were flown against targets on Failaka Island. Improved weather allowed for the completion of all planned sorties on the 22nd (20 sorties) and 23rd (40 sorties).

'On 24 February we were woken at 0300 hrs and told that the ground war to liberate Kuwait had started', explained Col Hancock. 'We would now fly actual CAS missions in support of Marines and Coalition forces. The next few days would pass quickly as the situation in Kuwait rapidly changed. We now had the full support of everybody on the ship. At this point the Navy was doing a fantastic job, as everyone was excited about having a far more personal role in the war. Morale was extremely high all round.

'Prior to the ground war commencing, we could be more careful and more selective in our attack profiles. With Marines now on the ground fighting the Iraqis in direct combat, you would do whatever you had to do to put bombs on the target. This was certainly the case in the mission I flew on 27 February, on what would prove to be the last shooting day of the war. We checked in with the Marine DASC, which used the call-sign "Chieftain". We were assigned a target at coordinates 30 degrees, 06 minutes north/47 degrees, 43 minutes east, and told to contact "Combat 05", a Marine F/A-18D working as a FastFAC. The target was described as multiple vehicles and revetted positions.

Posing with two VMA-331 AV-8Bs on the deck of LHA-4 prior to the start of hostilities, Maj Ben Hancock flew his fair share of training sorties while embarked. '*Desert Storm* started without VMA-331 and *Nassau*. The amphibious task forces' mission wasn't really clear at that point, and we were held for a possible amphibious assault or as reserves to replace frontline casualties', Hancock recalled. VMA-331 flew no fewer than 2838 training sorties while operating from *Nassau* during this deployment (*Ben Hancock*)

'We switched over to the frequency that "Combat 05" was working. I asked for a pilot weather report and enemy threat report. "Combat 05" reported that weather was about 10,000 ft overcast and visibility about seven miles. There were reports of AAA in the area. At this point we were still over the Arabian Gulf, headed north at 28,000 ft, and I read back the coordinates to my three wingman and they all acknowledged with their flight numbers. We then closed up and began to descend, breaking out at about 6000 ft. Continuing to head north, we soon went "feet dry" over Kuwait. We were about 15 miles north of Kuwait City, and the visibility here was poor due to the black smoke from the burning oil wells.

'I took time to pull out the map and plot the target. It was just north of the Kuwaiti border in Iraq, near Safwan. This would be our first time in Iraq, so I told the guys to be "heads up". We were now flying at 450 knots ground speed in our standard division formation, with "Peewee" flying in loose fighter wing off me and "Woody's" section in trail in combat spread. This put both aircraft abeam each other at about a mile apart, thus allowing each pilot to check his wingman's "six" – the blind area behind the jet.

'We could hear "Combat 05" working a section of F/A-18s onto some targets, and the FastFAC told us to hold about ten miles south of the target until we were cleared in. My "spider sense" was tingling because were being highlighted below the clouds above us. At our altitude we were in easy range of almost all enemy ground-to-air threats. We were also going to attack desperate, retreating, Iraqi soldiers in the same area where other jets had just stirred them up with bombing and strafing runs. They would be looking for us.

'At last we were cleared onto the target by "Combat 05", who was going to mark it on the ground for us. Just prior to rolling in we heard several abort calls, and "Combat 05" told us to circle west for our attack. We were at 8000 ft doing 480 knots, and I started a hard left turn away from the highway as I strained to keep my eyes on the target. We rolled out, heading southwest, and I was about to roll in heading southeast when "Mystic" yelled "Break, Break, Flares!" I strained under the g forces and looked around frantically as multiple SAMs were in the air. At least two were streaking toward "Woody". One hit him in the left exhaust nozzle of his jet, right below the wing. He yelled "I'm hit, I'm hit", and pulled up into the clouds trailing black smoke.

'The missiles had been launched from our "seven o'clock" and were on us in seconds. "Mystic" had one chasing him as he disappeared from sight into the clouds. Fortunately, the heat-seeking missile chasing "Mystic" could not track him through the overcast.

'He radioed "Woody" to turn his jet to the southeast. "Woody's" last transmission was "I can't control it!" For what seemed like an eternity, but was probably only 20 seconds, "Peewee" and I looked in a northeastly direction until we saw "Woody's" jet impact the ground in one huge, orange ball of flame. It was like watching a slow motion movie, but this was the real thing. We never saw a parachute. We dropped our bombs on a dump target and flew back to *Nassau*.

'After landing back on the ship my jet was chained down and I just sat there, feeling numb. We had been scheduled for three missions that morning and the war wasn't going to slow down for us. "Mystic" asked me to lead the three of us on a second mission. I felt apprehensive about that only because I feared losing another wingman, but "Mystic" and "Peewee" insisted that I lead, so I did. The weather was getting worse by the hour, and we were forced to drop our bombs on positions on Bubiyan Island. At 0400 hrs the next day a ceasefire came into effect and the war was over. The Iraqis had been forced out of Kuwait.'

On 27 February the 'Bumblebees' had flown 47 of their scheduled 60 missions, but had suffered the loss of AV-8B BuNo 162740. Its pilot, Capt Reginald C Underwood, was killed in action.

During *Desert Storm* VMA-331 had become the first AV-8B squadron to successfully operate from an amphibious assault ship in combat. The 'Bumblebees' had demonstrated the capability to sustain nearly 60 sorties in a single day of operations. VMA-331 pilots flew a total of 242 combat sorties totalling 269 flight hours, and delivered more than 250 tons of ordnance – 775 Mk 82s, 66 Mk 83s, 64 Mk 20 CBUs and 10,171 rounds of 25 mm cannon ammunition.

Following the end of hostilities, the squadron continued training operations until it finally returned to MCAS Cherry Point on 17 April 1991. As part of the Cold War

Having just landed back aboard LHA-4 following a training mission, the pilot is marshalled towards the stern of the vessel, where his Harrier II will be chained down to the flightdeck (*US Navy*)

Sailors arm and prepare an AV-8B of VMA-331 on one of *Nassau's* elevators following the unit's commitment to *Desert Storm* on 20 February 1991. The squadron flew 242 combat sorties and delivered more than 250 tons of ordnance, with one combat loss. Two jets were also destroyed and a pilot killed in operational accidents (*Peter Mersky collection*)

drawdown that followed *Desert Storm*, VMA-331 was deactivated on 1 October 1992.

VMA-513 DETACHMENT BRAVO

With Saddam showing no sign of removing his forces from Kuwait, US and Coalition governments began moving additional forces to the Arabian Gulf from November 1990. 5th MEB, based in California, was amongst the reinforcements ordered to the region, with transport being provided by the US Navy's ARG 3. MAG-50 was the aviation force assigned to 5th MEB, and it consisted primarily of reserve units. A third of VMA-513 – known as Detachment Bravo – with six AV-8Bs embarked aboard USS *Tarawa* (LHA-1), while the rest of the unit headed to the Far East to maintain defence commitments in this region.

VMA-513 'The Nightmares' can trace its heritage back to February 1944, when it was commissioned as Marine Fighter Squadron 513 and equipped with F6Fs. It flew these fighters into combat off the escort carrier USS *Vella Gulf* (CVE-111) in the Pacific during the final months of World War 2. The unit also saw action in the Korean War as VMF(N)-513, conducting nightfighter operations with the F4U-5N Corsair and F3D Skynight (the latter from mid-1952). Based in Japan from 1953 to 1962, flying F4D Skyray fighters, 'The Nightmares' moved to MCAS El Toro, California, and re-equipped with F-4B Phantom IIs as VMFA-513 in 1962. The unit completed a single combat tour in South Vietnam in 1965, after which it was posted to MCAS Cherry Point. In 1971, the squadron re-equipped with the AV-8A Harrier, which VMA-513 flew until its 1987 conversion to the more capable Harrier II.

Maj (later Lt Col) Georges 'Bone' LeBlanc served as second-in-command of VMA-513's Detachment Bravo;

'When Iraq invaded Kuwait in August 1990, I was serving with Yuma-based VMA-513. I had just returned from a normal peacetime six-month WESTPAC deployment aboard USS *Peleliu* (LHA-5). In October, VMA-513 was notified that a squadron detachment of six Harrier IIs and associated personnel was to embark aboard *Tarawa* and deploy to the Middle East in support of contingency operations. We joined the vessel on 30 November and began the month-long transit to the Arabian Gulf. I was assigned as the Assistant Officer in Charge, and performed the roles of Operations Officer and Senior Landing Signal Officer for the detachment.

'En route, we began reading the mission reports from Harrier II units already in-theatre. It became immediately evident that our tactical training, based upon a

An aircraft from VMA-513's Detachment Bravo lands aboard *Tarawa* during *Desert Shield*. Capt Tom Carnesi, who flew with the Det, recalled 'Recovery aboard "the boat" during the day was relatively easy, but landing at night in a Harrier II had a high "pucker" factor. An unaided night approach to the boat was the most difficult thing I did in the Harrier II, and that includes flying combat missions!' (*The Boeing Company*)

high-threat Iraqi integrated air defence system, would not address the threats – small arms, AAA of all sizes and hand-held SAMs – that our sister squadrons were expecting to encounter in the KTO once combat commenced. I knew that we needed to retrain quickly while still underway.

'With the AV-8B's ability to load "simulated" ordnance into the weapons delivery system, which in turn gives the pilot the HUD symbology that real bombs and missiles would, we developed an abbreviated training syllabus to realign our tactics. Using our task force ships as targets (since nothing else was available at sea), the syllabus proved very effective.

'Once in-theatre, and after participating in Operation *Sea Soldier IV* in late January and early February 1991, we transited into the Arabian Gulf and prepared for an amphibious landing into Kuwait – which turned out to be a diversion. During this period, we were anxious to "get into the fight" but were not included on the ATO. Because of this, we were restricted from conducting combat operations. Despite significant effort, we continuously failed to be included on the ATO, and in the war. Additionally, we discovered that the mere transmission of the ATO to amphibious shipping at sea was a major problem. This meant that had we been able to get onto the ATO, we would not have been able to see it!

'Finally, on 14 February, and without warning, we were told that the Detachment was to disembark and join other Harrier II squadrons stationed at King Abdul Aziz Naval Base. The aircraft were flown off and the ship pulled into Al Jubail Naval Base to unload our personnel and supplies. Detachment Bravo was flying combat sorties within 48 hours.

'We were briefed upon arrival that our primary mission was to conduct BAI against artillery and other enemy weapons systems in Kuwait. On one occasion, however, 1Lt Tom "Vito" Carnesi and I got to fly an emergency CAS mission. We checked in with "Chieftain", who in turn passed us on to "Rhino", a ground FAC. We were each carrying four Mk 82 high explosive conical finned bombs and 300 rounds of 25 mm cannon ammunition.

'I checked in with "Rhino", whose unit was in contact with a well dug in Iraqi force in the Al Wafra oilfield in southern Kuwait. When he keyed the mike, we could hear the fire fight in the background. He told me that he had an immediate CAS mission, and passed us a standard nine-line CAS brief with a four-minute time on target "hack". When I plotted the target coordinates, however, I noticed that they were behind us in Saudi Arabia! I told "Rhino", who re-transmitted the correct coordinates, and added two minutes to the "hack" time. We pushed from the control point in combat spread at 15,000 ft.

'Once we were in the target area the FAC illuminated the Iraqi position with laser energy and I rolled in, leaving "Vito" to provide high cover. I was experiencing heavy small arms fire from the trench line occupied by the enemy, and as I approached my pull out altitude I had still not achieved a laser lock, so I broke off my attack and "Vito" rolled in. He never managed a lock either, so I told him to pull off low at a height of 8000 ft and I re-attacked from a different axis. Re-attacks were pretty much forbidden unless there were Marines in contact, which they were

This view of King Abdul Aziz Naval Base was taken from the soccer stadium. VMA-513 Detachment Bravo was sent to the facility in mid-February, as Maj Georges LeBlanc explained. 'On the 14th, without warning, we were told we were to disembark from *Tarawa* and join the other Harrier II squadrons at King Abdul Aziz as part of MAG-13 (Forward). The aircraft were flown off and the ship pulled into nearby Al Jubail to unload personnel and our supplies. We were flying combat missions within 48 hours of our arrival' (*The Boeing Company*)

All six VMA-513 Detachment Bravo aircraft bask in the warm sunshine on the ramp at King Abdul Aziz following their recent departure from *Tarawa*. The Det's pilots were assigned to VMA-311 for day-to-day support and operational tasking during *Desert Storm* (*Peter Mersky collection*)

in this case. This time I got a laser lock and released my bombs. As I pulled off, and as "Vito" rolled in, the FAC transmitted, "Hit lead's smoke. His bombs are right in the trench line." "Vito" did exactly that and pulled off for the 130-mile flight home. As we left the target area "Rhino" said, "Thanks a lot. They are not shooting anymore."'

1Lt (later Lt Col) Thomas Carnesi had only recently joined VMA-513 when Iraq invaded Kuwait;

'My two roommates at Yuma were assigned to VMA-311, and they deployed immediately after the invasion. At that time, VMA-513 was not assigned to support the build-up of forces for *Desert Shield*. In October the unit was ordered to deploy to MCAS Iwakuni to assume duties as the UDP Harrier II squadron. At the same time VMA-513 was told to provide a six-aircraft detachment to deploy with MAG-50 aboard *Tarawa*. Maj Ed Holcomb was designated as the officer-in-charge of VMA-513 Detachment Bravo and assigned the required six jets, as well as 90 Marines. We formed the detachment in early November and accomplished pre-deployment training in daytime carrier qualification. Our detachment consisted of ten pilots and one augment pilot from Marine Aviation Weapons and Tactics Squadron 1, Maj Kevin "Hulk" Conyers. Our detachment was well manned with experienced pilots who had just returned from the WESTPAC 90 deployment on LHA-5. Our maintenance department was also experienced following this cruise.

'As MAG-13 and the Marine Corps transitioned from the A-4M to the AV-8B, VMA-513 carried the brunt of the shipboard deployment burden

Sailors and Marines line the deck of the amphibious assault ship USS *Tarawa* (LHA-1) as it sails into Pearl Harbor, Hawaii, on 1 May 1991 whilst returning home to San Diego from *Desert Storm*. The ship left the USA on 1 December 1990 with a detachment of six AV-8Bs from VMA-513 embarked (as well as CH-46Es, CH-53Es, AH-1Ws and UH-1Ns). The Harrier IIs operated from the vessel in the Arabian Gulf until they were sent ashore to King Abdul Aziz Naval Base on 15 February 1991 (*US Navy*)

on the west coast. As of 1990, VMA-513 was a fully operational AV-8B unit and VMA-311 was just completing its transition. VMA-211 and VMA-214 were in the process of transitioning from the Skyhawk to the Harrier II night attack and were not yet operational. Overall, thanks to the LHA-5 cruise, I would say that VMA-513 Det Bravo was both well manned and trained for the combat deployment. All pilots were at least qualified section leads, with many of us division leads or better.

'Having embarked on *Tarawa* on 30 November, 5th MEB sailed from San Diego the following day. The other aviation ship in our amphibious ready group was USS *New Orleans* (LPH-11), which embarked many of MAG-50's rotary-winged assets. Also in the ARG were numerous "small decks" (LSD/LPD), which could operate a limited number of rotary-winged assets. We docked in Pearl Harbor and Subic Bay on the way to the Arabian Gulf. Both stops were to bring more Marines aboard, as well as to pick up supplies. We reached the Arabian Sea on 7 January 1991, where we rendezvoused with 7th MEB and its ARG. During this time it was not uncommon to see US amphibious ships dotting the entire horizon.

'In the lead up to *Desert Storm* it was determined that Det Bravo needed to have a night capability. Four pilots, including myself, were designated as "night guys", and we began a night training syllabus. Usually, this consisted of training at an airfield, then a land-based simulated LHA deck, culminating in night qualification at the ship. Due to no shore-based facilities being available, we were briefed on night operations and then launched in the "pinkie" period after dark, where we could still see. We went directly into a night period and were qualified as night pilots.

'Recovery aboard the "boat" at night in a Harrier II has a high "pucker" factor. Basically, you fly a Carrier-Controlled Approach (CCA) to a spot about 0.8 nautical miles behind the "boat". Throughout this approach it is pitch black. Your only outside references are a few ships' lights bobbing in the distance. Once you are guided onto the proper heading and glide slope by the CCA controller, you begin to pick up "the ball". This visual glide slope reference is reassuring. Coming down the glide slope, you set the jet up in landing configuration (gear/flaps), as well as deflect the nozzles down to 50-60 degrees to achieve slow flight. The aeroplane is now developing half its lift from the engine and the other half from the wing, although it still flies like a conventional aircraft.

'At around 0.8 nautical miles you begin to "fly the ball" as your primary reference, while you bring the nozzles into hover stop (fully deflected down) position. This begins a delicate dance of fuel management and ship closure speed. You don't want to be too fast crossing the stern of the ship or you won't be able to stop and land at the appropriate spot. On the other hand, you don't want to slow down too much and chase the ship, as most of the time you are dependent upon water injection for hover performance, and that is limited by the amount of water carried by the aircraft (usually less than 60 seconds' worth).

'Combine this with the natural tendency for the Harrier II to require increased engine power during the transition to hover flight (so as to make up for the loss of wing lift as you decelerate) and you've got a handful to manage! Can't be too fast, but can't be too slow, can't be too high and not too low. Watch the water gauge click toward zero. Most of the time you don't have enough fuel to try a second approach. It's hairy! An unaided night approach to the boat was the most difficult thing I did in the Harrier II, and that includes flying combat missions!'

Overcrowding of the flightdecks available to air assets within the amphibious task forces and the realisation that a major amphibious assault was not likely eventually resulted in VMA-513 Detachment Bravo being sent ashore to King Abdul Aziz on 15 February. Here, the Det joined up with VMA-311 and became part of MAG-13 (Forward). 5th MEB was in turn re-designated I MEF reserve, and on 24 February its ground combat and support elements landed at Al Mish'ab, in Saudi Arabia, in support of Joint Forces Command East.

'Our six-aeroplane detachment was brought in to replace Harrier II losses to that time', explained Lt Col Carnesi. 'We were assigned to fly with VMA-311, our sister MCAS Yuma squadron. They flew combat missions with us as wingmen so as to get us ready. As a junior guy in my Det, I really did not have knowledge of the "big picture". Our mission was to prepare the battlefield for the ground invasion. Daily ops were similar to all the Harrier II squadrons in-theatre.

'Conventional flight in the AV-8B was straightforward. The aeroplane had good acceleration and power at lower altitude, although performance fell off the higher you went due to the design of the high-bypass Pegasus engine. The AV-8B's total ordnance load-out was somewhat limited compared to other platforms in-theatre such as the F-15E or A-6E, although its ability to put bombs on target made up for this lack of quantity. A typical load during *Desert Storm* was four to six Mk 82s or Mk 20 Rockeye IIs, plus the 300 cannon rounds.

'Utilising the ARBS, we were able to acquire and lock up targets using visual contrast (day only) and feed this information into the mission computer, where the data was crunched into release parameters. These were presented to the pilot in the HUD, allowing us to drop our ordnance on the correct aim points. One of my lasting impressions of the combat missions I flew in *Desert Storm* was how similar they were to our training sorties back home on the ranges near Yuma.'

Despite its late arrival, VMA-513 Detachment Bravo made a solid contribution to the air war, flying 103 strike sorties during *Desert Storm* and suffering no combat damage or losses. At the end of the conflict, 5th MEB remained in the region as residual forces afloat, and it was sent to support humanitarian relief efforts following a cyclone in Bangladesh. VMA-513 Det Bravo did not return home until the end of June.

VMA-231

VMA-231 'Ace of Spades' is one of the oldest Marine Corps squadrons, being able to trace its history back to 1919. The unit fought across the Pacific in World War 2 but was eventually deactivated in 1962. It was resurrected at MCAS Cherry Point in 1973 and equipped with AV-8As, thus becoming only the second squadron in the Marine Corps to receive the Harrier. VMA-231 switched to the AV-8B in 1985-86. In June 1990 the squadron deployed to Japan for a WESTPAC tour, replacing VMA-542. Col (then Lt Col) W R 'Rusty' Jones led the unit at the time;

'We were temporarily stationed at NAS Cubi Point, in the Philippines, from Iwakuni when Iraqi forces invaded Kuwait. We, as well as the rest of MAG-12, fully expected to be sent to the Arabian Gulf. These expectations were quickly dashed when we were informed that we would remain in WESTPAC. Ultimately, the experience gained by VMA-231 during the WESTPAC UDP tour proved to be invaluable when the unit subsequently redeployed to Saudi Arabia. While awaiting the order to move, we focused on training up the low-time pilots in VMA-231 so as to expand their skills set in the AV-8B.

'Finally, over the Thanksgiving weekend in late November, we got the message to head to the Arabian Gulf. We immediately started packing, as well as camouflaging our jets ghost grey using paint acquired from the Hornet squadrons that were co-located at Cubi Point. Having painted the aircraft ghost grey overall, we then took another can of ghost grey and mixed in a cup full of black paint to make a darker shade of grey. This was sprayed over sections of the jet to create a grey/dark grey camouflage scheme. We also painted the intakes gloss white. The Harrier II's large intakes looked like black dots when viewed head-on, but the gloss white paint removed the previously conspicuous shadow.

'We departed Cubi Point on 8 December and met our KC-10 tankers en route to Wake Island, where we spent a night, then flew on to MCAS Kaneohe Bay, in Hawaii, where we again overnighted. It was then on to MCASs Yuma and Cherry Point. Some of our jets broke down along the way, with one having tanking problems, another being forced to spend the night at Iwo Jima and two aircraft diverting to Midway for 24 hours. Shortly after leaving Kaneohe, one of my wingmen suffered a fuel probe leakage in his jet that meant he couldn't take on gas. He had to return to Hawaii and get the probe tip changed. The stragglers just kept on flowing from wherever they had been forced to stop, and, depending on who you were and when you got there, we had from one to four nights at Cherry Point prior to launching for Saudi Arabia.'

The deployment order saw VMA-231 travel 18,000 miles in 14 days as it redeployed to Saudi Arabia to join MAG-13 (Forward). During the theatre switch VMA-231 flew no fewer than 904 hours in two weeks – a record for a Harrier II fleet squadron. Once in-theatre the aircraft were ready for action within several days of their arrival.

VMA-231 CO Lt Col 'Rusty' Jones takes on fuel from a KC-10A in 'Shank 01', complete with its one-off 'sharksmouth'. He recalled, 'We flew out and met the KC-10s and spent a night in Wake Island, a night in Kaneohe and a night in Yuma, before pressing on to Cherry Point. I gave my pilots the order to "Just get up and go". Depending on who you were, and when you got there, we had from one to four nights in Cherry Point before we launched for Saudi Arabia' (*'Rusty' Jones*)

A VMA-231 jet tanks from a KC-10A somewhere over the Pacific during the unit's long trip from Japan to the USA and then on to Saudi Arabia. The deployment order saw the squadron travel 18,000 miles in 14 days, moving from MCAS Iwakuni, back to the USA to prepare and then on to King Abdul Aziz to join MAG-13 (Forward) (*Andrew Hall*)

Amongst the pilots to complete this redeployment was Col Anton Nerad, then a first lieutenant;

'I was the CO's wingman when we launched from Rota on 22 December. We found King Abdul Aziz without too much difficulty and landed. The landing itself was eerie as there was sand blowing across the runway. It looked like snowdrifts, and it was something that I had not seen before. We parked the jets and covered them up in an attempt to keep the sand out.

'It was exciting to be there, operating alongside two squadrons of Harrier IIs and two OV-10 units. The base was pretty crowded, and every single pilot and officer from VMA-542 was out on the ramp to greet us upon our arrival. I remember getting out of my jet and seeing guys I knew from Cherry Point. They gave me a "near beer" and welcomed us. We were allocated space in the soccer stadium in which to build our ready room, and we started flying pretty much straight away.

'We were initially paired up with VMA-542 guys, who showed us the border area, current medium altitude tactics and defensive concepts against the Iraqi threat in the KTO. We discussed the jet's RWR and bolt-on jamming pod, plus medium altitude tactics, flying around in the desert haze and the local command-and-control procedures. We learned quickly, and when the weather was clear we did well with the ARBS and general target detection. The challenge with the ARBS was the heightened workload for the pilot when using it. Indeed, it took quite a bit of effort from the pilot to get the equipment's mechanisation to work correctly. Some pilots were better at it than others, with a number of guys simply using the barometric bombing method. Good hits could be achieved with both methods. However, the ARBS was deadly accurate, and it gave the AV-8B unprecedented capability at that time.'

1Lt David Vosteen also served with the 'Ace of Spades' in *Desert Shield/Desert Storm*;

'When I tell people I flew the Harrier II, I inevitably get asked the question "Was it hard to fly?" V/STOL is different, but in a good way. The avionics in the jet were excellent. Even back in 1990, the software was eye watering. If properly managed, the INS kept a pretty accurate position. It could load up to 26 waypoints, which made navigation a piece of cake. The HUD was awesome for someone coming straight out of a TA-4J in training. In flight, the AV-8B was as solid as a rock, the thick wings keeping it stable at low altitudes and in a dive.

'It was also a great bomber, as the air-to-ground systems were pretty accurate. Using systems deliveries, we routinely hit within 50 ft of a target from an 8000-ft release altitude. The day attack AV-8B was only one thing – a bomber. The ARBS was an awesome piece of bombing gear, being very accurate. In fact, thanks to this system the Harrier II was statistically more accurate than the F/A-18 in *Desert Storm*. We also had a Laser Spot Tracker (LST) built into the ARBS, which I used a couple of times during the conflict. Unfortunately, the use of ARBS was not drummed into our heads enough before the war, resulting in many pilots using barometric pressure altitude when working out their dropping height above the target. This in turn meant that we weren't as good as we could have been at bombing during *Desert Storm*.'

Col Nerad recalled that VMA-231's XO, Maj Donald E Fleming, led the first section into combat once the air war commenced on 17 January;

'They were scrambled off alert, thus becoming the first "Ace of Spades" crews to fly a combat mission in an AV-8.

'Like other Harrier II units, once the action started we relied on three basic loads for our jets – the most common was six Mk 82s, then four Mk 83s and finally six Mk 20 Rockeye IIs. Most of the time one of us in a flight had an AN/ALQ-164 jamming pod mounted on the centreline stores station. VMA-231 used six Mk 82s most of the time, and we also carried the cannon pods on jets not equipped with an ECM jammer.

'We used the gun in a number of ways. Sometime we would perform dedicated strafing runs, and other occasions we would simultaneously use the gun and drop bombs. A lot of pilots would roll in, shoot the gun and drop their bombs all in the one pass. Other times, we would just roll in from medium altitude and strafe a target. I do not recall seeing a single aeroplane with only strakes fitted in place of the gun at any stage in the conflict, as the weapon proved to be very reliable.

'We saw a lot of AAA – grey bursts of 57 mm and darker 85 mm. Sometimes you did not see it. Indeed, after one mission I told our intel

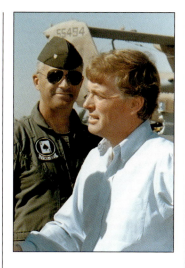

Vice President Dan Quayle was given a tour of King Abdul Aziz Naval Base on 31 December 1990. Standing behind him in this photograph is Lt Col 'Rusty' Jones, CO of VMA-231 (*'Rusty' Jones*)

A VMA-231 AV-8B fires its GAU-12 25 mm cannon during a training mission in the late 1980s. This image shows the substantial muzzle blast that was created when the gun was used. 'We also carried the 25 mm gun on every mission', explained Col Russell Sanborn. 'It was very effective, and you could shoot the gun and drop bombs at the same time – I liked that. It may have been ineffective from medium altitude, but in my mind it would keep the enemy's heads down and maybe I would get one or two lucky kills with the gun. During the dive I would hold the trigger down for the full 300 rounds of high explosive incendiary (HEI), then "pickle" my bombs' (*'Rusty' Jones*)

folks that we had not been shot at, only to see orange balls of AAA flying by the nose of my jet when we replayed the HUD tape! I guess I was looking out the side of the aircraft at the time, rather than out the front.

'The frustrating thing was that we did not know how we were doing in the war overall. The Iraqis were not stupid, and they hid their artillery, rockets and tanks with sand. They also employed numerous decoys that looked like real targets from the altitudes that we were flying at. Our training could also have been better when it came to picking out a real target from a fake one. We did not get a lot of BDA or general feedback on our efforts. We just knew we were blowing up a lot of stuff, and doing our best. History tells us that we did indeed do a good job, but we did not know that at the time. I am sure that we could have done a lot better had we known what effect our bombing was having on the enemy.

'The schedule kind of flowed out. You would be scheduled twice a day. Fly one mission, refuel and rearm, fly again and be done for the day. The next day you were scheduled a bit later, so one day you might fly at night and the next in the day. Your schedule changed, but we needed to have at least two jets available around the clock. I ended up flying many night strikes, and they weren't fun. You had to work with a FAC, and sometimes you got target illumination from flares, or used ambient light.

'During day missions we occasionally got to use a MULE LST (the AN/APQ-3 Modular Universal Laser Equipment, which was a hand-held target locator and guide for laser-seeking projectiles used by Marine Corps ground FACs and FAC(A)s – the AV-8B had an LST in the ARBS to detect coded laser illumination on the ground). I preferred Rockeye IIs for BAI missions, followed by Mk 83s and, finally, Mk 82s. The Mk 83s were very accurate, as they went where you wanted them to go.

'The other thing about the Harrier II day attack aircraft was that these jets only had the 65 percent leading edge wing root extensions (LERX). These created vortices over the wing surface that in turn enhanced manoeuvrability. When we normally dove, we went down at a 60-degree angle to get a better look at the target, thus ensuring a closer spread of weapons. That high-dive angle resulted in a really accurate release. The only problem was that after you pickled your bombs, with the small LERX and original F402-RR-406 motor, the jet took a long time to climb back up to a safe altitude. It seemed like an eternity until we reached 15,000 ft. When you released your bombs at 8000 ft and pulled back on the stick, you could see the wings visibly rocking – that is what the 65 percent LERX did. So you would be wobbling around back and forth, pitching the nose up and climbing for all you were worth.'

The later AV-8B night attack aircraft and Harrier II Plus (which was fitted with radar) were equipped with the larger 100 percent LERX and a higher thrust Rolls-Royce F402-RR-408 turbofan engine. These significantly improved both the rate of turn and rate of climb.

'Initial operations were fraught with "growing pains" at all levels', Col 'Rusty' Jones recalled in his VMA-231 Command Chronology for January 1991. 'Very few of the command and control agency personnel had combat experience, and the amount, and detail, of direction from above varied greatly in those first weeks.

'A real frustration for the pilots was the delivery restrictions surrounding the Mk 20 Rockeye II when dropped by the AV-8B. Due to software programme limitations, computed weapons delivery symbology for the CBU was not normally displayed in the HUD above 8000 ft under normal attack parameters. I initially directed the carriage of Mk 20s to assist the MAG in its husbanding of Mk 80 series bombs.

'As the pilots rightfully pointed out, the rules of engagement for *Desert Storm*, which stated that strike aircraft had to stay above the AAA and SAM threat, and the carriage of a weapon that precluded a high release, put them in a tactically untenable position. I relented and changed the daylight load to four or six Mk 82s and the night load to six Mk 20s.

'Early use of laser spots by both ground and airborne designators proved marginal at best. The lack of power output by the MULE (which relied on a portable battery) that was in service with the Tactical Air Control Parties, and the required target stand off distances observed by OV-10 crews, negated the use of the AV-8B's LST. Use of the laser all but guaranteed direct hits, however, so the squadron continued to press for laser spots for both day and night missions. Our early missions with the F/A-18D proved to be very frustrating too. As with other aspects of command and control in *Desert Storm*, VMFA(AW)-121 was also on the early portion of the learning curve.

'VMA-231 pilots flew an average of eight to ten combat sorties each between 17 and 31 January. Their professionalism allowed for flexibility while airborne when responding to tasking from the DASC and FAC(A).

'As shown in the daily ATO, Marine Air target priorities were threefold. First was the MEF target list. Each flight launched with a primary and secondary target assigned – usually artillery, an armoured unit or command post. Second was the utilisation of a FAC on the ground, but usually sat in the back of an F/A-18D or OV-10. The DASC could react to a Joint Tactical Air Request and direct an in-flight section to work with a FAC to hit a target of opportunity or another high priority target. Thirdly, the ATO could identify a "kill box" that allowed a flight to utilise armed reconnaissance techniques to locate and attack Iraqi units within a 15 x 15-mile square area. Once airborne, the flight had a high chance of executing an attack given the priorities described.'

Maj (later Lt Col) Don Fleming, who served as VMA-231's executive officer during *Desert Storm*, commented;

'At first we tried to fly missions with four to eight jets. I recall a mission where we flew as assigned by the ATO against a target just north of the border. However, when we got there the Iraqis had moved. They were not going to wait in the same place and get bombed, so they moved a lot at night or under the cover of smoke from the fires they had set. On the way back, I tried to rendezvous with the rest of the formation. We would return home low so as to allow the jets heading north to go in high.

'I started a left turn and kicked out a few flares so that my pilots could see me. Then I saw an aircraft 180 degrees out, but it was a very pointy jet like a Mirage F 1 or MiG-23, not an AV-8B. I converted to his "six" and set up my one AIM-9M. We had been briefed that the IrAF's basic tactic was to fly in trail so that if you went after the lead, the trailer would bag you. I levelled my wings and looked. Sure enough, there was another jet. I turned to convert on No 2. However, something told me not to shoot unless I knew for sure it was an enemy. I let them go and they disappeared in the haze. I wanted to be a Harrier II guy who got a kill, but I did not want to shoot down a Free Kuwait or French jet.

'There is a funny thing that happens during combat. You start to see and hear better and you learn more quickly. It is hard to explain, but it happens. You become more aware of things occurring on the ground. For example, on one mission that I can recall we had used all our bombs to destroy our primary target – a series of buildings – but we still had our guns and gas, so we flew further south into the kill box to look around. We were at medium altitude – 15,000 ft – and I saw something different on the desert floor. I could

Capt Michael 'Killer' Kelly conducts his pre-flight walkaround checks of 'Shank 02' during the first week of *Desert Storm* ('Rusty' Jones)

not clearly make it out, so I dove down to take a look. At 6000 ft I clearly saw vehicle tracks. I looked back up and spotted my wingman still circling at 15,000 ft.

'Following the tracks south, I eventually saw a company of Iraqi BMP armoured personnel carriers (APCs) well hidden in the shadows of a Kuwaiti police station near to the Saudi border. The new tracks had betrayed their location. As I went down to strafe them I called the DASC and told them to get a FAC(A) over here so that we could do a target hand off. My wingman and I circled overhead the police station until an F/A-18D joined us. Its crew quickly saw what I saw and called in other jets to target the BMPs.

'Eventually, the whole Harrier II wing adopted a sort of "kill box" mentality. This is where American pilots are at their best, being able to operate in a decentralised manner. We took a load of bombs to an area and we would patrol over it at a certain time and meet up with a FAC(A) in an F/A-18D who would direct us to targets. I recall one FAC(A) that was getting harassed by AAA from positions right along the coast. He got my eyes on the target, which was a battery of S-60 guns. We took

An aerial view of the 'Ice Cube Tray', which was a noted Kuwaiti landmark used as a reference point by F/A-18D FAC(A)s when directing AV-8B pilots to targets over the KTO (*Andrew Hall*)

them out for him, as well other targets. If there was no FAC(A) available you found targets for yourself. We had a shopping list – artillery, armour, command posts, troops and defensive positions. We were cleared to drop on anything we thought had target value within the strict parameters of our assigned kill box.'

Capt (later Lt Col) Andrew Hall was another Harrier II pilot to see considerable action with VMA-231 in *Desert Storm*;

'We had slick Mk 82s and 500-lb bombs fitted with Snakeye retarding fins, the latter weapons having come off the MPSs. The ordnance crews banded the fins so that they would not pop open, thus allowing us to use them like regular bombs. Squadron armourers would decide which bombs were to be loaded on each pylon after checking with the aircraft's weapons computer. The ballistics for the various ordnance cleared for use by the AV-8B was stored in the jet's central computer.

'The slick Mk 82s were spot on, and one could generally expect a hit with them. However, the mil dispersion of the Mk 82 with banded Snakeye fins was significantly higher because of the additional drag. They were universally disliked by pilots because of their inherent inaccuracy compared to the conventional-finned Mk 82s. We must have had a lot of surplus Snakeye fins that someone had decided we had to use up. We usually dropped the bombs two or four at a time, and occasionally one of the straps on a banded Mk 82 would break or come lose after release. The fins would open and the bomb would fall very short of the intended target. We also had Mk 83 1000-lb bombs, although I dropped very few of these. I dropped some Mk 77 napalm too, but most of my strikes were with Mk 20 Rockeye II CBUs.

'The Mk 77 was not overly popular since we had to deliver it at low altitude, and it had significant dive limitations. I think it required a 20-degree or less dive angle, and its accuracy was poor since it was shaped like a keg of beer. When the Mk 77 came off the aeroplane it flopped around so it was not a particularly accurate weapon. We used these bombs just before and during the ground war to ignite oil pools around Iraqi fixed defences

VMA-231's 'Shank 13' taxies out for a strike during the early stages of *Desert Storm*. The aircraft is armed with Mk 20 Rockeye IIs and AIM-9M Sidewinder missiles, the latter only being carried during the first week of the air war when the IrAF still posed a potential threat to strike aircraft over the KTO (*The Boeing Company*)

Capt Bill 'Bull' Delaney and his CBU-toting AV-8B at King Abdul Aziz during *Desert Storm*. Having flown 35 missions during the conflict, Delaney was killed on 10 August 1993 at MCAS Cherry Point when his AV-8B (BuNo 162955) crashed during a touch-and-go evolution (*Andrew Hall*)

Capt Andrew Hall poses in front of a VMA-231 jet that has also been armed with Mk 20 Rockeye IIs. 'Most of my strikes were with CBUs', Hall told the author. 'Sometimes, we would carry both Mk 82s and Rockeye IIs so that we could go after a wider set of target types. We did this a lot in the second half of the air war, when we were often going to kill boxes unsure of what we would be attacking' (*Andrew Hall*)

and to cause general unease among the ground forces.

'Very few Laser Mavericks were fired as we needed a platform to illuminate the target with laser energy for them to work properly. Our Marine A-6s had laser designators, but they were busy doing interdiction strikes. The Hornet FAC(A)s didn't have them either, so the guys that used Laser Mavericks had their targets designated for them by ground FACs. The fact that we did not have stocks of the IR Maverick like the USAF A-10 units was a source of great frustration for our pilots, as we really could have used that weapon.

'Sometimes we would carry both Mk 82s and Rockeye IIs so that we could go after a wider range of target types. We did that a lot in the second half of the air war when we were often sent to kill boxes without knowing exactly what it was we would be attacking.

'Even during day missions, with the AV-8B you required good visibility to see and then hit your targets. There were many poor visibility days in Saudi Arabia, Kuwait and southern Iraq, when the sand was blowing in the air or the humidity was high. If you were on the early morning launch during the war, often you would go up and not be able to see a thing on the ground due to sand, fog or the angle of the sun. Later, after the Iraqis blew up the oil well heads, there was always black smoke in the air, which caused big problems.

'I liked the way my CO summed up the situation. "Don't go out there and hang it out just to be tough. That does not make any sense. We need to conserve our people and assets." As long as our guys were NOT in contact – this was before the ground invasion – he did not want the pilots to do anything foolish, and if they did so, they got a talking to.

'During the ground war, if guys were in contact and in immediate need, we had to get beneath the clouds to deliver weapons. I recall that on a couple of missions we came in at about 7000-10,000 ft and hung around over the battlefield. Being silhouetted against the overcast layer was a really bad position to be in. I did it, but I was very uncomfortable. However, the guys on the ground needed us to do our job, so you had to be there. We had to assume a higher risk profile than normal.

'The Iraqis generally did not see you, or know that you were coming, until the first bomb detonated. Then everyone ran out to their AAA guns and started pumping rounds up into the air – mostly 57 mm AAA. We would see RWR indications of radar control for AAA, so we knew that they were looking at us. For radar SAMs, the RWR would let us know that we were being seen by the target tracking radar for the SA-2. Some guys reported the target tracking radars from the SA-6 as well. A few even saw unguided SA-2/6 missiles, and I personally had an SA-2 guidance indication but with no missile launch observed.

'To their credit, the Iraqis tried to hit us with what they had, but it was not very effective. What was effective was firing a shoulder-launched or vehicle-mounted IR missile at a jet as it climbed out. I believe that one of our guys was hit by a vehicle-fired SA-9 and the rest by shoulder-launched SA-7/14/16 IR SAMs. They were so hard to see when fired.

'During our training and preparations for the air war, we invited an air defence officer from Egypt – they were a part of our coalition against Iraq – to King Abdul Aziz to give us an operator's view on Iraqi air defence systems, capabilities and training. He had fought in the various wars with Israel using identical Soviet AAA and SAMs to those now fielded by Iraq in Kuwait, and his insight was both interesting and helpful when it came to figuring out what we were up against.

'One of our main dilemmas was whether to use pre-emptive flares or not. After an attack, should you put out flares as you climbed away, thus becoming visible to Iraqi gunners, or not, hoping instead that the bad guys hadn't seen you? We did not have a firm policy in VMA-231 because our CO left it up to individual pilots. I initially believed that one should not put out flares, but after a couple of our aircraft were shot down, I personally concluded that it was much better to put out flares to decoy the IR missiles than not. The flares were so effective and the shoulder-fired SAMs were so difficult to see.

'In retrospect, I feel that our RWR training was adequate, although we did not know as much about this equipment as we should have. The RWR was more than adequate for the threats we faced in the KTO, but we should have understood the system better. The AN/ALQ-164 jamming pod was fantastic against continuous wave and pulse radar threats such as the tracking units for SA-2/6 SAMs. Again, we had a basic understanding of how it worked too, but not enough knowledge. It weighed 500 lbs, and was like bolting a large fuel tank beneath the aeroplane due to the drag it caused. The latter soured the pilot's opinion of the store, which was a shame since it was an incredibly well engineered and effective piece of equipment. I now wish we had had one for every aeroplane in the early phases of the air war. We did not see a lot of radar-guided threats over southern Kuwait, but they were there. Since we did not have enough jamming pods, we generally gave it to the last guy in the formation on a strike mission. And he was certainly the most vulnerable.'

Lt Col Jones' Command Chronology report for February 1991 stated;

'As *Desert Storm* continued into February, the squadron maintained the pace set by the ATO. As the month went on, the threat from SAMs increased steadily. More SA-6 regiments were reported moving south and the number of unguided SA-8/9 firings increased. SA-7/14/16s were reported regularly by pilots from all squadrons. The high altitudes used for ingress, attack and egress all but negated the effect of the shoulder-fired systems. VMA-231 did not use the ALQ-164 DECM pods until the SA-6 threat increased during the first week of February.

'One factor of flying in Kuwait and Saudi Arabia that was truly unforeseen and appreciated by all was the amount of bad weather. Low visibility and ceilings were the rule rather than the exception as the war went on. As oil fires later increased, the addition of dense black smoke complicated battlefield support from the air.'

Capt (later Col) Russell Sanborn noted that the bombing tactics he used in *Desert Storm* were not overly dissimilar to those used by Marine Corps units in World War 2;

'You came in high, found the targets visually, rolled in with iron bombs, put a pipper on the target if it could be seen, dove and released your bombs, and then climbed back up to your altitude sanctuary. And you hoped your bombs hit the target. At this time you had to put a lot of iron down to kill targets. It was all Mk 82s and Rockeye IIs, and that was an issue since the latter were designed for low altitude delivery. We did not even have an algorithm for the computer in the aeroplane for Rockeye II deliveries above 10,000 ft at that time.

'We would simply ingress at 15,000-20,000 ft and roll in on the target, despite aiming symbology not appearing on the HUD for placement over the target until you passed through 12,000-10,000 ft! The HUD symbology would appear once the aircraft mission computer had calculated the information – usually only in the last seconds of your dive. Having hastily made corrections to your angle of attack, you then dropped your bombs.

'When calculating the optimum release point for your ordnance, the computer had taken into consideration the aircraft's motion, wind data and weapons ballistics, after which it gave you corrections for all these so as to achieve effective bombing. If all the data was not correct for the bombs, or the Rockeye IIs did not open at the correct time of flight, the weapons missed the target. So the rule of thumb was that we would typically carry six Mk 82s on the AV-8B. We knew that one bomb would kill a tank, but only if you directly hit it, or any other target you were aiming at. We were not overly accurate bombers at this early stage in the AV-8B's frontline career, hence we carried six weapons and were told to drop all of them on the target in the hope that maybe one or two would strike home. The technical aspects of bombing were laid out for us in the Joint Munitions Manuals.

'The Harrier II is streamlined, and carrying 3000 lbs of ordnance on the jet is not a problem. We also had the 25 mm gun pods fitted for every mission. My maintenance guy always said to me "You use it all the time." The gun was very effective, and you could shoot it and drop bombs at the same time. I liked that. It may have been ineffective from medium altitude, but in my mind it would keep their heads down, and maybe I would get one or two lucky kills with the gun. In the dive, I would hold the trigger down and fire all 300 rounds, then

Burning oil wells in Kuwait fill the air with smoke during the final days of *Desert Storm*. 'With the day attack AV-8B you required good to reasonable visibility when attacking targets, even during daytime', noted Capt Andrew Hall. 'Later, after the Iraqis blew up the oil well heads, there was always black smoke in the air, and it caused us big problems.' VMA-231 remained in Saudi Arabia and flew sorties over Kuwait until its departure on 15 March 1991 (*'Rusty' Jones*)

A maintainer from VMA-231 inspects a Rolls-Royce Pegasus F402-RR-406 engine following its removal from 'Shank 10'. To keep the dust out, most engine maintenance was performed in the portable hangars to the left of the flightline at King Abdul Aziz (*'Rusty' Jones*)

let go of the trigger and pickle my bombs. I was carrying the ordnance so I felt that I should use it all. I told my maintenance guys "If you are willing to load it, I am willing to release it."

'The Rockeye II proved to be a lot draggier than the Mk 82, but it was a better weapon for killing artillery in a revetment or tanks and APCs. To kill a revetted target like an artillery tube or tank with a Mk 82, you had to have a CEP (circular error probability) of 15 ft or so. With Rockeye II you just had to get close to the target, as you had 247 bomblets per canister or 1482 bomblets per full load on an AV-8B. The bad news with the bomblets hitting sand was that they had a ten to fifteen percent dud rate. In fact when I got shot down I recall seeing white Rockeye canisters on the desert floor. For every one that I could see, there were 30 or so unexploded bomblets per canister buried in the desert sand just waiting for me to step on them.

'The other thing that was far from satisfactory with the day attack variant of the AV-8B was that it only had room for 60 chaff and flare expendables. These did not last very long in a combat situation. You can drop a lot of chaff and flares from when you roll in until the time you pickle your bombs and get back up to the altitude sanctuary. VMA-231's Weapons and Tactics Instructor told me that the standard tactic was to save your chaff and flares until you had been highlighted coming off target. It was believed that such a tactic gave you the greatest chance of defeating IR SAMs, as you did not exhaust your supply of chaff and flares before they were most needed. I got shot down because I followed this general rule, however.

'We would dive on our targets from high altitude, which in turn meant that the Iraqis could not

Having received a re-supply of CBUs, more 25 mm ammunition (note the gunpowder residue that has stained the cannon pod fitted to 'Shank 16', BuNo 163686) and a top up of fuel, these aircraft are manned up prior to undertaking yet another KTO mission (*Andrew Hall*)

'Shank 08', assigned to Capt Greg Gaff during the campaign, completed 39 missions in *Desert Storm*. The mission tally was applied to the aircraft within a small black bomb marking that was stencilled onto the port side of the fuselage to the right of the 'Ace of Spades' emblem. Each VMA-231 jet bore such a marking, as well as two lines of Arabic script immediately above the 'bomb' – these were applied to the aircraft shortly after the ceasefire came into effect (*Andrew Hall*)

see us. Thus, we did not put out flares until we came off the target. We would roll in from 15,000 ft and drop our bombs at between 12,000 and 10,000 ft. The jet would bottom out near 8000 ft, at which point the enemy would usually see us and open fire. So, we would generally put out flares whilst climbing back up toward 15,000 ft. I followed this tactic as briefed, choosing not to put out my flares coming down the chute, and I got hit coming off target.

'I was shot down over the KTO on 9 February whilst undertaking my 17th mission. Flying as "Jump 57", I came in on the target – bunkers and artillery – from medium altitude (15,000-18,000 ft) as "Dash 2" for Col Bioty. We were working with an F/A-18D FastFAC, who had just marked the target. I rolled in, shot the gun, pickled my Mk 82s and pulled up. As I was climbing, I rolled out to look for the bomb impact. They had not yet hit, so I rolled wings level. That was when I was struck by the SAM. Later, intel told me it was probably an SA-16 that hit me after working an analysis from the altitude at which I was hit and the speed I was travelling at at the time.

'There was a loud thump and the missile blew up on the hot left nozzle, taking out part of the left wing, including the left flaps. The aeroplane flipped upside down and was spinning violently, and all the "Bitching Betty" cockpit warning lights and audio tones were going off – she was telling me "engine fire, hydraulics", like I didn't know! The jet was spinning faster and faster like a corkscrew. I wasn't flying any more, just sat in an out-of-control jet for about 15 seconds. I knew I had to get out. I remember the canopy shattering away, the fire from the rockets underneath the seat, the seat itself actually riding up the rail and me being ejected. All of it happened automatically, which was a good thing as I passed out when I ejected from the G forces. I got bruises on my feet from hitting the cockpit on the way out and burns from the rocket motor on the back of my neck. All of that was minor compared to what could have happened to me! I was alive.

'It was a violent ejection, and I woke up about 10,000 ft above enemy territory after I had just dropped six Mk 82s on Iraqi positions. It was extremely quiet, with the wind noise in my helmet as I drifted down. Seconds earlier I was talking on the radio and had all of the loud noises of a jet aircraft in combat, then the crash of the missile impact and now near silence. It was eerie, and I was now drifting. I thought to myself "This will not be a good day."

'Whilst I was in the parachute I followed my training. I pulled out my survival radio, put the earpiece into my helmet and set the radio on frequency 282.8 MHZ. From that altitude I had a five- or six-minute ride to the ground. I used all that time to get ready. I talked on the radio to tell Col Bioty or the FastFAC that "Jump 57" had just ejected from an AV-8B, and I was

The cost of war. US and Kuwaiti troops inspect the burnt out remains of Capt Russell Sanborn's AV-8B BuNo 162081, which was downed by an IR SAM over the KTO on 9 February 1991 (*The Boeing Company*)

alive and well. I had been trained as a FAC and done a FAC tour, and I knew what to do once I hit the ground. I was ready to call for air support to prepare for a rescue.

'When I landed, I spread out my orange and white parachute as a marker. I was hoping that someone would talk to me on the radio, and we would put up a restricted zone to where I could call in air support. However, no one ever talked to me on the radio and the emergency locator transmitter never went off – it was supposed to activate when the seat was ejected. Neither system worked. Was my equipment defective or were they damaged in the ejection? We will never know. My radio turned on but all I heard was static. Neither Col Bioty or the FastFAC saw me get hit by the SAM or float down in the parachute. After the war, Col Bioty apologised for not seeing me. The only report they had was seeing a 'chute on the ground a short while later and a smoke plume, but they did not know if I was alive or dead. Once we got about four miles apart that was the limit of seeing anything. Col Bioty kept calling me on the radio and looking around, but when he hit bingo gas, he had to go home.

'My plan was to bury myself in the dirt, hide my parachute and walk away from the crash site in the dark. Shortly after I had landed I saw a dozen Iraqis with AK-47s coming my way. My mind was racing on adrenalin from being shot down and thinking about how to escape. When I saw those guys coming over the hill, I thought, "My gosh. My radio does not work and my 9 mm pistol is not going to outshoot a bunch of angry soldiers with AK-47s". I called on the radio, "This is 'Jump 57'. I am alive and about to be captured". They walked right up to me and took away the radio. They were yelling at me to put my hands up. I was on the ground for only about 20 minutes before I was captured. I would subsequently be at the mercy of the Iraqis for 26 days.

'The soldiers took my stuff away down to my flight suit, and we walked to an underground command post bunker. I met the guy who claimed to have shot me down and he took my name tag. I was wearing a green flight suit that day as my tan one was dirty. I then went to the battalion HQ, where I was roughed up pretty good by the "C team" – one of them accidentally discharged his AK-47 and got yelled at. I was then taken in a truck to a higher HQ, where I was run through a gauntlet of soldiers.

An aerial image of Iraqi vehicles destroyed by air strikes along the main Kuwait to Basra road, dubbed the 'highway of death' by Coalition pilots. MAG-13 (Forward) assets targeted this area in the final days of *Desert Storm* (*'Rusty' Jones*)

They yelled, screamed and spat at me, and I was also hit with their rifle butts. I fell down and they picked me up and made me run through them again. I thought I was going to die. They were like rabid dogs. Most of the Iraqi troops looked bad – some wore blue jeans and others a mix of fatigues and civilian clothes. Only a few had a full uniform. They all had beards and looked scruffy. These were not frontline troops.

'I was driven to another place at night, perhaps Basra, and then north to Baghdad. As we moved

AV-8Bs sit ready to depart after being rearmed and refuelled at Tanajib. Maj Don Fleming, who served as XO of VMA-231, recalled 'We could take off, fly north, bomb the Iraqis and then land at the forward operating base at Tanajib, which was only 23 miles south of the border' (*Andrew Hall*)

Pilots and senior support troops of VMA-231 come together at King Abdul Aziz just prior to the unit's departure for home. During the conflict, the 34 officers and 175 enlisted personnel of VMA-231 worked as a team, conducting 987 combat sorties for a total of 1195 flying hours. During these missions the pilots delivered 1.6 million pounds of ordnance, including 1660 Mk 82s, 62 Mk 83s, 969 Mk 20 Rockeye IIs and 78 Mk 77 napalm bombs, as well as firing 22,709 rounds of 25 mm ammunition (*'Rusty' Jones*)

at night in the dark the driver would hastily pull off to the side of the road whenever jets were heard close by. I worried that we would get an IR Maverick through the side of the truck, but we got to Baghdad okay. I was taken to the prison within Al-Rashid military camp on the southern outskirts of Baghdad, where Saddam kept political and mentally ill prisoners. It was a regular prison with cell blocks, bars, cement floors and walls, with a little tiny window way up high. There was a foam pad on the floor with one blanket and a bucket in the corner for a bathroom. At night, when we bombed Baghdad, the guards would disappear into their bunkers and we could whisper to neighbouring cellmates across the hall. David Lock, a truck driver, was across from me – he was wounded – and three British SAS guys, one whom later wrote the international bestseller *Bravo Two Zero*, were two cells down. I shared the latest info about the war with them, bringing them up to speed on how it was progressing.'

Along with the other Coalition PoWs, Capt Sanborn was finally released into the hands of the International Red Cross on 6 March 1991.

Maj Don Fleming told the author that the AV-8B was a success in *Desert Storm* because of its short take-off and landing capabilities;

'We operated 86 jets in Saudi Arabia only because we were flying from a field no other jet could fly from. You could land a Harrier II on the dilapidated runway next to the soccer stadium, rearm, refuel and take-off again in short order, thus achieving a really high sortie rate that kept the

jet over the KTO virtually round the clock.

'The AV-8B had good legs, and I never had to midair refuel. We could go up to the Kuwait City area with 4000 lbs of bombs, hang around for 20 minutes and still bring our ordnance home if required. We could take-off, fly north, bomb the Iraqis and then land at the forward operating base at Tanajib, which was only 23 miles south of the border. Here, we could get something to eat and drink while the troops refuelled and rearmed the jets, and be back over the Iraqis an hour after we had left the KTO. They must have gotten real sick of that since there were always Harrier IIs flying overhead, targeting them with bombs, CBUs and cannon rounds. We had amazing versatility.'

At 0800 hrs on 28 February 1991 offensive operations ceased, and according to VMA-231 CO, Col 'Rusty' Jones, 'the CG (Commanding General Lt Gen Walter Boomer) called the MAG CO (Col John Bioty) to say he was elated with MAG-13 (Forward). There was no elation on the part of the Marines of VMA-231, however. A kind of cautious relief overcame everyone.'

During the conflict, the unit's 34 officers and 175 enlisted personnel had worked as a team and conducted 987 combat sorties totalling 1195 combat flight hours. During these missions the pilots had delivered 1.6 million lbs of ordnance, including 1660 Mk 82s, 62 Mk 83s, 969 Mk 20 Rockeye IIs and 78 Mk 77 'fire' bombs, and expended 22,709 rounds of 25 mm ammunition.

VMA-231 remained at King Abdul Aziz for a further two weeks after the conflict had ended, flying a handful of training and BDA assessment sorties over Kuwait. Preparations were soon underway for the return trip home, and on 15 March 19 VMA-231 jets departed for Rota, tanking from KC-10 tankers en route. On the 18th the unit's aircraft, and three AV-8Bs from VMA-542, landed aboard USS *John F Kennedy* (CV-67) and rode the carrier back across the Atlantic – they reached MCAS Cherry Point on 27 March.

On 15 March 1991 VMA-231 aircraft flew, with KC-10 tanker support, to Rota. Three days later, following a single field carrier landing practice period per pilot, 19 Harrier IIs from VMA-231 flew out to the aircraft carrier *John F Kennedy* and landed aboard for the ride home. Three AV-8Bs from VMA-542 shared deck space with VMA-231 aboard CV-67, the 'Tigers'' remaining aircraft being embarked in USS *Saratoga* (CV-60) (*Rusty Jones*)

Capt Bill Delaney flies VMA-231's 'Shank 03' back to MCAS Cherry Point on 27 March 1991, having taken off from *John F Kennedy* when the vessel was some 200 miles off the eastern seaboard of the USA (*Andrew Hall*)

APPENDICES

AV-8B HARRIER IIs INVOLVED IN OPERATIONS *DESERT SHIELD/DESERT STORM*

VMA-231 'ACE OF SPADES'

162081*, 162943, 162944, 162962, 162964, 162967, 162972, 162973, 163183, 163426, 163514, 163515, 163662, 163665, 163670, 163673, 163682, 163686, 163687

* shot down by IR SAM on 9 February 1991, Capt Russell A Sanborn PoW

VMA-311 'TOMCATS'

163176, 163181, 163194, 163517, 163518*, 163519, 163660, 163661, 163664, 163668, 163669, 163672, 163674, 163675, 163680, 163681, 163683, 163684, 163688, 163690

* shot down by IR SAM on 28 January 1991, Capt Michael C Berryman PoW

VMA-331 'BUMBLEBEES'

162074, 162076, 162080, 162082, 162083, 162085, 163126, 162722, 162726, 162728, 162731, 162736, 162737, 162738, 162740**, 162743***, 162788, 162948, 162953, 162954*

* operational loss on 22 January 1991, Capt Manuel Rivera killed
** shot down by IR SAM on 27 February 1991, Capt Reginald C Underwood KIA
*** operational loss on 19 March 1991, unnamed pilot rescued

VMA-513 'THE NIGHTMARES'

163178, 163192, 163193, 163203, 163204, 163420

VMA-542 'TIGERS'

161573*, 151575, 161584, 162069, 162945, 162946, 163179, 163188, 163190**, 163197, 163198, 163199, 163201, 163206, 163421, 163424, 163425, 165516, 163663, 163676

* either shot down by IR SAM or flew into the ground on 23 February 1991, Capt James N Wilbourne KIA
** shot down by IR SAM on 25 February 1991, Capt Scott Walsh rescued

AV-8B COMBAT LOSSES

28/1/91 (Monday) VMA-311 – Initial notification of aircraft shot down by a suspected SA-9 or SA-14 shoulder-launched IR SAM was at 1010 hrs. Pilot, Capt Michael C 'Ras' Berryman, was flying BuNo 163518 (Tail Number 'WL 02') as 'Cat 37', with flight lead Capt 'Sprout' Hines. No parachute observed and no emergency beacon seen or heard. AAA observed in the vicinity. Capt Berryman was thought to be a fatality, but at war's end he was listed on an International Red Cross report as a 'captive' and was released on 6 March with the other American PoWs.

9/2/91 (Saturday) VMA-231 – Capt Russell 'Bart' Sanborn, flying BuNo 162081 (Tail Number 'CG 09') as 'Jump 57' with flight lead Col John Bioty Jr, call sign 'Hunter'. Pair were attacking artillery emplacements in the vicinity of N290220 E473610 at the time. Parachute observed but no emergency beacon or radio transmissions subsequently heard. Capt Sanborn was taken prisoner soon after descending to the desert floor. Jet hit by either an SA-7 or SA-14 IR SAM after pull-off from target. Unit heard via the International Red Cross that Capt Sanborn was a PoW, and he was released on 6 March with the other American PoWs.

23/2/91 (Saturday) VMA-542 – Initial notification of aircraft down was at 2020 hrs. Pilot, Capt James 'Trey' Wilbourne, was flying BuNo 161573 as 'Pride 16', his flight lead being Capt Dan 'Salt' Peters. Both men were attacking targets and troop emplacements just north of Ali Al Salem airfield at night. Lead observed his wingman roll in and release bomb/s (Mk 83s), and then saw ordnance detonating on the desert floor. A second (large) explosion was then seen just north of the initial bomb impact point. Distinct possibility that Capt Wilbourne's aircraft was either hit during the roll-in/dive or the pilot simply flew into the ground – disorientation or departure from controlled flight was highly suspected, but could not be confirmed. The pilot's remains were later recovered.

25/2/91 (Monday) VMA-542 – Capt Scott Walsh, flying BuNo 163190 as 'Jump 42', was hit by an SA-7 or SA-14 IR SAM. His flight lead was Cap Dan 'Salt' Peters. Aircraft was hit in the vicinity of N291500 E0473700. Capt Walsh attempted to get his AV-8B home, but a fire light came on in the cockpit and his controls then went stiff. Flight lead closed up on him and he saw significant damage to Capt Walsh's aircraft. An attempt to land at Al Jaber airfield in Kuwait (now in friendly hands) was made, but the undercarriage would not come down. An attempt to blow the gear down was then made, but only the nose gear and main gear dropped down – outriggers remained up. At about 600 ft, on a deep 180-degree turn, the aircraft pitched 50 degrees nose down and Capt Walsh ejected. He had a good parachute, was picked up by friendly forces and returned to base. Aircraft impacted two miles south-southwest of Al Jaber airfield.

27/2/91 (Wednesday) VMA-331 – Capt Reginald Underwood, flying BuNo 162740 (part of a flight of four AV-8Bs from *Nassau*), was downed by an SA-7 or SA-14 IR SAM near Safwan, Iraq. His remains were later recovered.

COLOUR PLATES

1
AV-8B BuNo 163517 of VMA-311, King Abdul Aziz Naval Base, August 1990
This aircraft was delivered to VMA-311 on 3 October 1988 as B-131. It was repainted at MCAS Cherry Point in 'grey-on-grey' camouflage before deployment, and is shown here in the ferry configuration (fitted with two 300 US gallon drop tanks and a pair of AIM-9Ms) used in August 1990 when the unit deployed to the Middle East in support of Operation *Desert Shield*. The wing, tail and other components of this aircraft were combined with a new fuselage, engine and other parts to create AV-8B Harrier II+ BuNo 165429 in September 2000.

2
AV-8B BuNo 163663 of VMA-542, King Abdul Aziz Naval Base, November 1990
This aircraft was delivered to VMA-223 on 30 November 1988 as B-138. VMA-542 took over VMA-231's aircraft upon the unit's return from Japan in mid-1990. The jet was repainted in 'grey-on-grey' camouflage at MCAS Cherry Point prior to deploying to Saudi Arabia, and it is shown here in standard *Desert Storm* configuration, armed with three banded Mk 82 Snakeye bombs on each of the wing pylons. The aircraft is also equipped with a relatively rare AN/ALQ-164 DECM jamming pod on its centreline. The wing, tail and other components of this aircraft were combined with a new fuselage, engine and other parts to create AV-8B Harrier II+ BuNo 165428 in August 2000.

3
AV-8B BuNo 163668 of VMA-311, King Abdul Aziz Naval Base, December 1990
This aircraft was delivered to VMA-311 as B-143 on 14 March 1989. It too was painted with 'grey-on-grey' camouflage at MCAS Cherry Point prior to deployment, and it is depicted here in a standard alert configuration as used for the first week of the air war. The wing, tail and various components of the aircraft were joined with a new fuselage, engine and other parts to create AV-8B Harrier II+ BuNo 166287 (the penultimate remanufactured AV-8B) in July 2003.

4
AV-8B BuNo 162731 of VMA-331, USS *Nassau* (LHA-4), Arabian Gulf, December 1990
This aircraft was delivered to VMA-542 as B-48 on 10 April 1986. It was later reassigned to VMA-331, repainted in 'grey-on-grey' camouflage at MCAS Cherry Point and embarked in *Nassau* with the 'Bumblebees' for Operation *Desert Shield/Desert Storm*. The aircraft subsequently served with VMAT-203 during the 1990s. The wing, tail and components of this jet were joined with a new fuselage, engine and other parts in January 2000 to create AV-8B Harrier II+ BuNo 165421.

5
AV-8B BuNo 163673 of VMA-231, King Abdul Aziz Naval Base, December 1990
This aircraft was delivered to VMA-542 as B-148 on 7 June 1989. When VMA-231 deployed to WESTPAC in June 1990, it took over VMA-542's aircraft at MCAS Iwakuni. All the Harrier IIs were repainted in Japan using a hand-mixed light grey/darker grey camouflage, and the aircraft is shown here in ferry configuration. In December 1990 VMA-231 aircraft flew three-quarters of the way around the world from Japan to King Abdul Aziz, via the USA, to reinforce MAG-13 (Forward). The wing, tail and other components of this jet were joined with a new fuselage and engine in August 2000 to create AV-8B Harrier II+ BuNo 165428.

6
AV-8B BuNo 163664 of VMA-311, King Abdul Aziz Naval Base, January 1991
This aircraft was delivered to VMA-311 as B-139 on 22 November 1988. It was repainted in 'grey-on-grey' camouflage at MCAS Cherry Point and flown to Bahrain in August 1990. On the morning of 17 January 1991, Maj Cary Branch flew BuNo 163664 in the first strike made by AV-8Bs in *Desert Storm*. In June 2002 the wing, tail and components from this aircraft were combined with a new fuselage, engine and other parts to create AV-8B Harrier II+ BuNo 165584.

7
AV-8B BuNo 163686 of VMA-231, King Abdul Aziz Naval Base, January 1991
This aircraft was delivered to VMA-542 as B-161 on 24 August 1989. As previously noted, when VMA-231 deployed to WESTPAC in June 1990 it took over VMA-542's aircraft in Japan. Repainted in hand-mixed light grey/darker grey camouflage, the aircraft is depicted here with a mixed load of AIM-9M Sidewinders and Mk 20 Rockeye II CBUs. Completing 54 combat sorties during *Desert Storm*, BuNo 163686 subsequently served with VMAT-203 post-war.

8
AV-8B BuNo 162074 of VMA-331, USS *Nassau* (LHA-4), Arabian Gulf, January 1991
This aircraft was delivered to VMA-331 as B-23 on 28 March 1985. It was repainted in 'grey-on-grey' camouflage at MCAS Cherry Point before deploying aboard LHA-4. Depicted here carrying a single Mk 83 1000-lb bomb under each wing, the aircraft later flew with VMA-231 prior to its wing, tail and components being joined with a new fuselage, engine and other parts in October 1997 to create AV--8B Harrier II+ BuNo 165311.

9
AV-8B BuNo 163665 of VMA-231, King Abdul Aziz Naval Base, January 1991
This aircraft was delivered to VMA-542 as B-140

on 2 December 1988. Taken on charge when VMA-231 deployed to WESTPAC in June 1990 and then repainted in the unit's hand-mixed camouflage, the aircraft flew 32 sorties and 36.9 hours in January 1991. Seen here armed with six Rockeye II CBUs, the jet later served with VMA-311. The wing, tail and components of this aircraft were joined with a new fuselage, engine and other parts in January 2002 to create AV-8B Harrier II+ BuNo 165580.

10
AV-8B BuNo 162954 of VMA-331, USS *Nassau* (LHA-4), Arabian Gulf, January 1991
This aircraft was delivered to VMA-331 as B-76 on 21 March 1987. Repainted 'grey-on-grey' at MCAS Cherry Point prior to deploying aboard *Nassau*, it was lost in a crash during a night training flight off the coast of Oman on 23 January 1991, killing Capt Manuel Rivera.

11
AV-8B BuNo 163518 of VMA-311, King Abdul Aziz Naval Base, January 1991
This aircraft was delivered to VMA-311 as B-132 on 4 October 1988. Painted in 'grey-on-grey' camouflage at MCAS Cherry Point prior to deployment, it is seen here in the attack configuration that was frequently used during the early stages of the air war. BuNo 163518 was shot down by an IR SAM during a strike mission over Kuwait on 28 January 1991, its pilot, Capt 'Ras' Berryman, ejecting successfully and becoming a PoW.

12
AV-8B BuNo 163662 of VMA-231, King Abdul Aziz Naval Base, February 1991
This aircraft was delivered to VMA-542 as B-137 on 18 November 1988 and turned over to VMA-231 when the unit deployed to WESTPAC in June 1990. 'Shank 01' was the squadron commander's jet, and as such it was adorned with a one-off 'sharksmouth' insignia and the nickname *VENOM* below the cockpit on either side of the fuselage. By the time *Desert Storm* ended on 28 February, BuNo 163662 had flown 54 combat missions totalling more than 65 hours. The mission tally was applied to the aircraft within a small black bomb marking that was stencilled onto the port side of the fuselage to the right of the 'Ace of Spades' emblem. Each VMA-231 jet bore such a marking, as well as two lines of Arabic script – free Kuwait – immediately above the 'bomb', upon their return to MCAS Cherry Point from Saudi Arabia in late March 1991. In June 2002 the wing, tail and components of this aircraft were joined with a new fuselage, engine and other parts to create AV-8B Harrier II+ BuNo 165586.

13
AV-8B BuNo 163421 of VMA-542, King Abdul Aziz Naval Base, February 1991
This aircraft was delivered to VMA-223 as B-122 on 22 July 1988. VMA-542 took over VMA-231's aircraft

when it returned to MCAS Cherry Point from Japan in mid-1990, and it deployed with these Harrier IIs to the Middle East. 'Lusty 01' was the squadron commander's aircraft, and it received a unique all-grey camouflage scheme and the nickname *Babieca* (the name of the horse ridden by 11th-century Spanish hero El Cid) during its time at King Abdul Aziz Naval Base. Reassigned to VMA-231 post-war, this aircraft was lost to a bird strike near Raleigh, North Carolina, on 15 October 1993.

14
AV-8B BuNo 162736 of VMA-331, USS *Nassau* (LHA-4), Arabian Gulf, February 1991
This aircraft was delivered to VMA-331 as B-53 on 9 May 1986. Repainted in a 'grey-on-grey' scheme at MCAS Cherry Point, it deployed to the Middle East aboard *Nassau*. Following the war, the jet served with VMAT-203 until it was lost following a midair collision with TAV-8B BuNo 164138 off the coast of North Carolina on 18 September 1995. The two-seat Harrier II landed safely, while the pilot of BuNo 162736 successfully ejected

15
AV-8B BuNo 163192 of VMA-513 Detachment Bravo, King Abdul Aziz Naval Base, February 1991
This aircraft was delivered to VMA-513 as B-107 on 9 March 1988. It was repainted in a 'grey-on-grey' camouflage scheme at MCAS Yuma prior to being embarked aboard *Tarawa* as a part of the six-aircraft Detachment Bravo on 30 November 1990. The jet was sent ashore from LHA-1 to King Abdul Aziz Naval Base on 15 February 1991, and it is depicted here armed with six Mk 83 'slicks'. The wing, tail and components of this aircraft were combined with a new fuselage, engine and other parts in May 2001 to create AV-8B Harrier II+ BuNo 165573.

16
AV-8B BuNo 162081 of VMA-231, King Abdul Aziz Naval Base, February 1991
This Harrier II was delivered to VMA-331 as B-30 on 3 July 1985. VMA-231 acquired the jet from VMAT-203 at MCAS Cherry Point during the unit's marathon deployment from Japan to the Middle East, BuNo 162081 replacing a 'broken' aircraft that had had to be left behind during the theatre move. 'Shank 09' had yet to be repainted in 'desert greys' when, on 9 February 1991, it was downed by an Iraqi IR SAM over central Kuwait. Capt Russ Sanborn ejected and was made a PoW.

17
AV-8B BuNo 163193 of VMA-513, King Abdul Aziz Naval Base, February 1991
This aircraft was delivered to VMA-513 as B-108 on 28 March 1988. It was repainted in 'grey-on-grey' camouflage prior to joining *Tarawa* as a part of the six-aeroplane Detachment Bravo. Post-war, this aircraft served with VMA-214 for much of the 1990s. The wing, tail and components were joined with a new fuselage, engine and other parts in January 2003 to create AV-8B Harrier II+ BuNo 165594.

18
AV-8B BuNo 163201 of VMA-542, King Abdul Aziz Naval Base, February 1991
This aircraft was delivered to VMA-223 as B-115 on 27 May 1988 and transferred to VMA-542 prior to the unit's commitment to *Desert Shield*. It is depicted here in a special anti-Iraqi defences attack configuration that saw the jet armed with Mk 77 napalm canisters. A small number of 'fire bombs' were dropped in hazardous low-altitude strikes in the KTO just before the ground assault commenced on 24 February 1991. Post-war, this aircraft served with VMAT-203 until it departed controlled flight and crashed during an air combat manoeuvring training sortie in the Virginia Capes Ops Area, off the coast of North Carolina, on 16 July 2003.

19
AV-8B BuNo 163680 of VMA-311, King Abdul Aziz Naval Base, February 1991
This jet was delivered to the VMA-311 as B-155 on 26 May 1989. The aircraft is also shown here armed with Mk 77 napalm canisters, BuNo 163680 being one of a small number of AV-8Bs assigned to clearing oil-filled Iraqi trenches just prior to the start of the Coalition ground assault on the KTO. The aircraft was stricken on 20 June 2001, although exactly what caused the airframe to be written off remains unrecorded.

20
AV-8B BuNo 163198 of VMA-542, King Abdul Aziz Naval Base, February 1991
This aircraft was delivered to VMA-223 as B-112 on 3 May 1988 and transferred to VMA-542 prior to deployment to *Desert Shield*. It is depicted here with an unusual mixed weapon load consisting of four banded Mk 82 Snakeye bombs and a pair of AGM-65E Laser Maverick missiles. Relatively few 'LMAVs' were used in Desert Storm by AV-8B units due to target designation problems – the Harrier II was not equipped with a laser targeting pod at this early stage in its career. The wing, tail and components from this aircraft were joined with a new fuselage, engine and other parts in October 2001 to create AV-8B Harrier II+ BuNo 165569.

21
AV-8B BuNo 163203 of VMA-513 Detachment Bravo, King Abdul Aziz Naval Base, February 1991
This aircraft was delivered to VMA-513 as B-116 on 6 June 1988. On 15 February 1991 VMA-513 Detachment Bravo was transferred to King Abdul Aziz Naval Base from *Tarawa* as attrition replacements for MAG-13 (Forward), the Det being paired up with VMA-311 until the end of the conflict. Post-war, this aircraft flew with VMA-211 for a number of years. Eventually, the aircraft's wing, complete tail section and components were joined with a new fuselage, engine and other parts in November 2001 to create AV-8B Harrier II+ BuNo 165578.

22
AV-8B BuNo 161573 of VMA-542, King Abdul Aziz Naval Base, February 1991
The very first production-standard AV-8B built by McDonnell Douglas, this aircraft was delivered to the Naval Air Development Center as B-5 on 14 November 1983. Flown by VMAT-203 during the early years of its career, BuNo 161573 was transferred to VMA-542 from this unit in August 1990 and repainted in 'grey-on-grey' camouflage at MCAS Cherry Point prior to deploying to the Middle East. It is shown here in standard *Desert Storm* attack configuration. BuNo 161573, and its pilot, Capt James 'Trey' Wilbourne, were lost in action over Kuwait on the night of 23 February 1991 while attacking targets and troop emplacements just north of Ali Al Salem airfield.

23
AV-8B BuNo 163204 of VMA-513, Detachment Bravo, King Abdul Aziz Naval Base, February 1991
This aircraft was delivered to VMA-513 as B-117 on 17 June 1988, and it deployed aboard LHA-1 with Detachment Bravo. BuNo 163204 saw action after coming ashore to King Abdul Aziz Naval base on 15 February 1991. After the conflict the aircraft served with VMA-211. The wing, tail and components of the jet were joined with a new fuselage, engine and other parts in November 2002 to create AV-8B Harrier II+ BuNo 165592.

24
AV-8B BuNo 162740 of VMA-331, USS *Nassau* (LHA-4), Arabian Gulf, February 1991
This aircraft was delivered to VMA-542 as B-57 on 28 July 1986. One of the jets taken by VMA-331 to the Persian Gulf aboard *Nassau*, it is depicted here equipped with an AN/ALQ-164 DECM jamming pod on its centreline. This aircraft, and its pilot, Capt Reginald C Underwood, were lost to an IR-guided SA-7 or SA-14 SAM near Safwan, Iraq, on 27 February 1991.

INDEX

References to illustrations are shown in **bold**. Plates are shown with page and caption locators in brackets.